# Code Red:
## Animals in Peril

# Code Red:
## Animals in Peril

A Supplement to
Childcraft—The How and Why Library

World Book, Inc.
a Scott Fetzer company
Chicago
www.worldbook.com

# Staff

For information about other World Book publications, visit our website at
**www.worldbook.com** or call **1-800-WORLDBK (967-5325).** For information
about sales to schools and libraries, call **1-800-975-3250 (United States),**
or **1-800-837-5365 (Canada).**

**Library of Congress Cataloging-in-Publication Data**

Code red : animals in peril : a supplement to Childcraft, the how and why library.
    p. cm.
    Summary: "An introduction to threatened animals and conservation, including
information about the kinds of animals that are in danger; why they are in danger;
and what people are doing to help them. Features include stories, drawings,
photographs, and a list of additional resources"--Provided by publisher.
    ISBN 978-0-7166-0626-0
    1. Endangered species--Juvenile literature.  2. Wildlife conservation--Juvenile literature.
I. World Book, Inc.  II. Childcraft.
QL83.C63 2011
333.95'22--dc22
                                        2011003061

World Book, Inc.
233 N. Michigan Ave.
Chicago, IL 60601
Printed in the United States of America
by RR Donnelley, Willard, Ohio
1st Printing April 2011

# Contents

**Vanished Animals of Long Ago** . . . . . . . . . . . . . . . . . . . . . . . . .8
Since the 1500's, more than 800 kinds of animals have become extinct. Among them
were such interesting creatures as the dodo, the sea cow, and the passenger pigeon.

**Vanishing Animals Today** . . . . . . . . . . . . . . . . . . . . . . . .30
Animals that have been the favorites of generations of children—the gorilla, the tiger, the
panda, the orangutan, and hundreds of others—are in serious trouble. Here is a look at the
ways of life and the problems of endangered animals in all parts of the world.

Africa . . . . . . . . . . . . . . . . . . . . . . . . . . . . . .38

Asia . . . . . . . . . . . . . . . . . . . . . . . . . . . . . .56

Australia . . . . . . . . . . . . . . . . . . . . . . . . . . . .74

Europe . . . . . . . . . . . . . . . . . . . . . . . . . . . . .86

North America . . . . . . . . . . . . . . . . . . . . . . . . .98

South America . . . . . . . . . . . . . . . . . . . . . .118

Oceans and Islands . . . . . . . . . . . . . . . . . . . .136

**Why Is It Happening?** . . . . . . . . . . . . . . . . . . . . . . . . . . .146
Wild animals are in danger because of too much hunting, because they are losing their
homes, and because people have sometimes tampered unwisely with nature. But throughout all the countries of the world, we are trying to solve the problems that have put so
many animals in danger.

**Helping Animals in Danger** . . . . . . . . . . . . . . . . . . . . . . . .182
Many people, from scientists to people who simply love animals, are doing what they can
to save all kinds of animals from extinction.

**What You Can Do** . . . . . . . . . . . . . . . . . . . . . . . . . . . .194
Some things you can do to help animals today.

**Find out More** . . . . . . . . . . . . . . . . . . . . . . . . . . . . . .200
Includes a list of books and websites for more information about animals and conservation
and the names of conservation groups you can contact to find out how you can help.

**Index** . . . . . . . . . . . . . . . . . . . . . . . . . . . . . . . . . . . . . . . .202

# Illustration Acknowledgments

The publishers of Childcraft gratefully acknowledge the courtesy of the following individuals and agencies for illustrations in this volume. When all the illustrations for a sequence of pages are from a single source, the inclusive page numbers are given. Credits should be read left to right, top to bottom, on their respective pages.

## Covers

Aristocrat, Discovery, International, and Standard Bindings: WORLD BOOK illustration by Anastasia Korochansckaja

Heritage Binding:
© age fotostock/SuperStock; © John Swanepoel, Shutterstock; © Exactostock/SuperStock; © Dreamstime; © Dreamstime; © Shutterstock; © Anita Huszti, Shutterstock; © F1 Online/SuperStock; © Dreamstime

Rainbow Binding: © Steve Bloom Images/Alamy Images; WORLD BOOK illustration by Matt Carrington

| | |
|---|---|
| 2–3: WORLD BOOK illustration by Anastasia Korochanskaja | 102–103: © Dreamstime |
| 8-9: © Carramba/Alamy Images | 104–105: © Merlin D. Tuttle, Bat Conservation International |
| 10–15: WORLD BOOK illustration | 106–107: © Rick & Nora Bowers, Alamy Images |
| 16-17: © Shutterstock | 108–109: © George H. H. Huey, Corbis |
| 18-19: WORLD BOOK illustration | 110–111: WORLD BOOK illustration |
| 20–21: © Image Asset Management/SuperStock | 112–113: © B. Moose Peterson, Ardea |
| 22-23: WORLD BOOK illustration | 114–115: © age fotostock/SuperStock |
| 24–25: © Bridgeman Art Library/Getty Images | 116–117: WORLD BOOK illustration |
| 26-27: © George H. H. Huey, Alamy Images; © Dreamstime; © Phil Savoie, Nature Picture Library; © Ronnie Howard, Shutterstock; © Karen Givens, Shutterstock; © blickwinkel/Alamy Images | 118–121: © Claus Meyer, Minden Pictures |
| 28–29: © Arcticphoto/Alamy Images; © Steven Kazlowski, Peter Arnold Images/photolibrary | 122-123: © Cusp/SuperStock |
| 30–31: © John Swanepoel, Shutterstock | 124–125: © Gabriel Rojo, Nature Picture Library |
| 32–37: WORLD BOOK illustration | 126–127: © Dreamstime |
| 38–39: © Duncan McKay, Alamy Images | 128–129: WORLD BOOK illustration |
| 40-41: © Minden Pictures/Masterfile; © F1 Online/SuperStock | 130–131: AP Photo |
| 42-43: © AWL Images/Masterfile | 132–133: © Minden Pictures/Masterfile |
| 44–45: © Martin Harvey, Peter Arnold Images/photolibrary | 134–135: © Dreamstime |
| 46–47: © Theo Allofs, Masterfile | 136–137: © Hal Beral VWPics/SuperStock |
| 48–49: © iStockphoto | 138–139: © Ron Niebrugge, Alamy Images; © Dreamstime |
| 50–51: © age fotostock/SuperStock | 140–141: © Tui De Roy, Auscape |
| 52–55: © Dreamstime | 142–143: © Ross Wanless |
| 56–57: © Tony Heald, Nature Picture Library | 144–145: WORLD BOOK illustration |
| 58–59: © Exactostock/SuperStock; © Minden Pictures/Masterfile | 146–147: © Shutterstock |
| 60–61: © F1 Online/SuperStock | 148–153: WORLD BOOK illustration |
| 62–63: © Dynamic Graphics 6/Jupiter Images/Creatas/ Alamy Images | 154–155: © Yann Arthus-Bertrand, Corbis |
| 64–65: © G. Tipene, Shutterstock | 156–157: © Tony Martin, WWI/Peter Arnold Images/ photolibrary |
| 66–67: © Anita Huszti, Shutterstock | 158–159: © Betty Press, Panos Pictures; © Minden Pictures/Masterfile |
| 68-69: © SeaPics | 160-161: © Uryadnikov Sergey, Shutterstock |
| 70-71: © Khoroshunova Olga, Shutterstock | 162-163: © iStockphoto |
| 72-73: © Shutterstock | 164–165: © Dreamstime |
| 74–75: © Dreamstime; © Ewan Chesser, Shutterstock | 166–167: © Gary Bell, Getty Images; © Darren J. Bradley, Shutterstock; © B. G. Smith, Shutterstock |
| 76–77: © Dreamstime | 168–169: © Shutterstock; © Dreamstime |
| 78–79: © age fotostock/SuperStock | 170–171: © Shutterstock; © Rosanne Tackaberry, Alamy Images |
| 80–83: © Dreamstime | 172-173: © Pacific Stock/SuperStock; © Angelo Gandolfi, Nature Picture Library |
| 84–85: © Jean-Paul Ferrero, Auscape | 174–175: © momentimages/SuperStock; © Shutterstock |
| 86–87: © Dreamstime | 176–177: © Dreamstime; © Minden Pictures/Masterfile; © Cal Vornberger, Alamy Images |
| 88–89: © Eric Isselee, Shutterstock; © age fotostock/SuperStock | 178-179: © age fotostock/SuperStock |
| 90–91: © Ivan Montero Martinez, Shutterstock | 180-181: David Silva, U.S. Coast Guard; © Joushua Wainwright, Alamy Images |
| 92-93: WORLD BOOK illustration | 182–183: AP Photo |
| 94-95: © blickwinkel/Alamy Images | 184–187: WORLD BOOK illustration |
| 96–97: © imagebroker/SuperStock | 188–189: © CBS/Landov |
| 98-99: © age fotostock/SuperStock | 190–191: © Newspix/Getty Images |
| 100-101: © Animals Animals/SuperStock | 192–193: The Raptor Trust |
| | 194–195: © Dreamstime |
| | 196–197: © Shutterstock |
| | 198-199: © Losevsky Pavel, Shutterstock; © Shutterstock |

# Preface

They squawked and squabbled and waddled about on rocky beaches. They swam in the cold waters of the ocean. Thousands of them lived on islands and along the coasts of the North Atlantic Ocean. They were big, 3-foot- (1-meter-) tall birds, somewhat like penguins. They were called great auks.

You have never seen a great auk and you never will. There are no longer any great auks on the islands and coasts where they once lived. There are none in zoos. There are no photographs of any. They were all killed by sailors who came to their islands and beaches and hunted them for food.

Could such a thing happen to any of the animals that are living now? Could it happen to the animals that you see in zoos, such as gorillas, tigers, and rhinoceroses? Could they someday be gone? Yes, that could happen.

At this very moment, nearly 9,000 different kinds of animals, in all parts of the world, are in very real danger. Scientists fear that many of them may soon be gone, just as the great auks are gone.

Which animals are in danger? Why are they threatened? Is there any hope for them? Can they be saved? Is anyone doing anything to help them?

You'll find the answers to those questions in this book—*Code Red: Animals in Peril.*

# Vanished Animals of Long Ago

*"Every creature is better alive than dead, men and moose and pine trees, and he who understands it aright will rather preserve its life than destroy it."*

**Henry David Thoreau**
Thoreau was an American writer of the 1800's who believed that people should live in harmony with nature. He is often considered America's first conservationist.

# The Last One

Makomo was on his way to the water hole to fill some pots when he saw the animal. He quickly hid behind some bushes to watch it.

The animal's hoofs made a *klop-klop-klop* sound on the hard, sun-baked ground. It trotted slowly toward the water hole, moving its head from side to side. It seemed to be sniffing the air. Perhaps it wanted to be sure that no hungry lion lay hidden nearby. When it came to the edge of the water hole, it lowered its head and began to drink.

Makomo was puzzled. He had never seen an animal like this one. It looked like a zebra, but its body was brown and its stripes were white. These stripes covered only its head and shoulders. What kind of animal could it be?

That night, Makomo told his father, Kama, about the strange new animal he had seen. What was it, he wondered. Where had it come from?

T. Chen

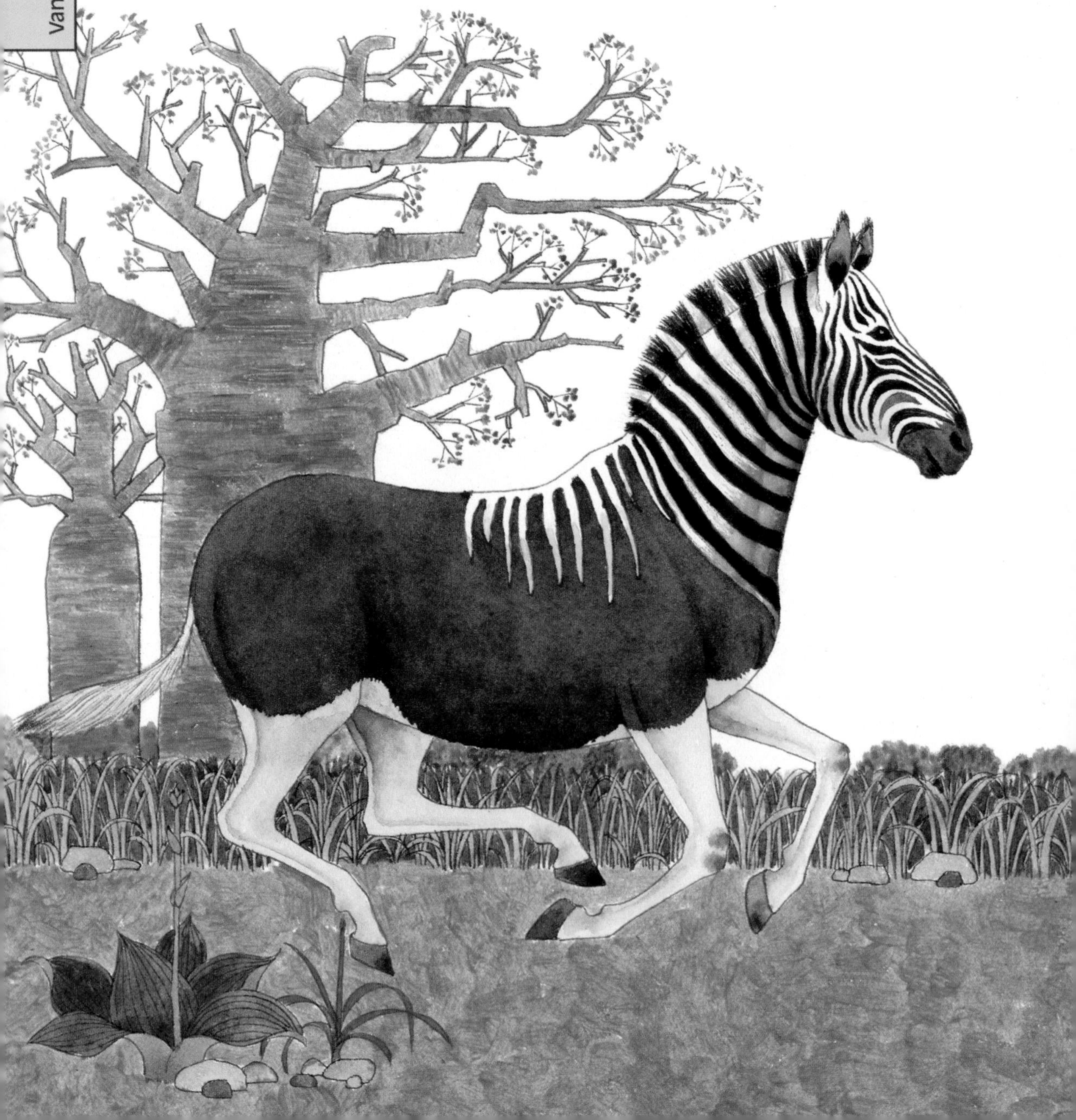

"I do not think it is a new animal from far away," said his father. "I think it is a quagga. When I was a little boy, as you are now, there were great herds of them in this land. But they have been gone for a long time. I did not think any were left."

"What happened to them?" asked Makomo.

"They were all killed," Kama replied. "The farmers shot them to feed their workers. They made bags of their skin, to put grain in. This quagga you have seen may be the last one."

Makomo thought about that. What would it be like to be the last one? How would he feel if he were the last person in the whole land? He would be lonely, he was sure. Was the quagga lonely?

Two days later, he saw the quagga at the water hole again. After that, he came every day to watch it. He squatted behind the bushes so that it would not see him and be frightened.

He came to know the quagga so well he could close his eyes and see it in his mind. Its coat was rich and shiny. Its eyes were brown, wise, and gentle. Its muzzle looked soft and velvety. He decided that it was the most beautiful of all animals.

He named it Beauty, and he talked to it in soft whispers. "One day I will let you see me, Beauty. But you will not be frightened. You will know that I mean you no harm. We will be friends. Then you will not be lonely any more."

And one day Beauty did see him. It had finished its drink and stood, head lifted, staring out over the plain into the setting sun. Abruptly, it snorted, turned its head, and looked straight at Makomo. It watched him for a long time. Then it snorted again. Tossing its head, the quagga raced off. Its hoofs drummed a song of wild freedom as it galloped away.

With shining eyes, Makomo watched it go. "When we are friends, Beauty," he whispered, "you will let me ride on you." He could not imagine anything more wonderful than to go flying across the plain on that brown, silky back.

Next day, Makomo did not hide. He sat in front of the bushes, without moving. The quagga came in sight, trotting steadily until it saw him. It stopped dead, watching him. He did not move. After a long time, the animal went to the water. It drank, pausing often to turn its head to look at him.

Each day, Makomo moved just a bit closer to the water hole. Always, he sat without moving a muscle, just watching while Beauty drank. At first, the quagga was nervous, but after many days, Makomo felt that it was getting to know him. It no longer paused when it saw him sitting near the water hole. The way it whisked its tail, tossed its head, and snorted was almost like a greeting. We are becoming friends, Makomo thought.

Then, one day, the quagga did not appear at the water hole. Makomo waited for it until the sun had set.

He went back the next day. Still there was no sign of Beauty. Worried, Makomo went to his father.

Kama looked at him sadly and placed a hand on his head. "He was an animal, my son, and every animal walks near death. It may be that a farmer shot him. Perhaps one of our own people speared him. Or, he may have been killed by a lion. It is even possible that he has gone back to where he came from. But I fear that he is dead. It happens, Makomo. Death is a part of life. This is something you must understand."

There was a hard, hurting lump in Makomo's throat. He knew that his father was right. He would never see Beauty again. He could never become its friend.

But there was something that made him feel even worse. If Beauty had been a zebra, or a gemsbok, or an eland, he would have felt sad, too. But there was a difference. There were many zebras and gemsboks and elands. Beauty had been the *only* quagga—the last one. Now there were none.

There are many kinds of animals, but none like a quagga. Beauty had been a special creature, just as each kind of animal is rare and special and unlike any other. The earth would never again feel the beat of a quagga's galloping hoofs. The sun would never again shine on a quagga's brown, silky coat. Makomo knew that he was not the only one who had lost something wonderful. So had the whole world.

A fossil skeleton of the dinosaur *Tyrannosaurus rex*, nicknamed "Sue," is on display at the Field Museum in Chicago.

# Why Are They Gone?

**B**eginning about 230 million years ago, dinosaurs roamed the Earth. They wallowed in great, green swamps and prowled through hot, damp forests in search of food. Some of them were the biggest animals that ever lived on land. Others were no larger than a chicken. There were dinosaurs with horns, dinosaurs with armored bodies, and dinosaurs with bills like ducks. For about 160 million years, these reptiles ruled Earth. Then, something happened. Nearly all the dinosaurs died out. They became extinct—a word that means that a whole group of living things is gone forever. (Since the 1960's, researchers have learned that birds descended from some kinds of small, meat-eating dinosaurs. Many scientists consider birds to be living dinosaurs.)

For a long time, scientists did not know why most dinosaurs became extinct. Did something terrible happen quickly or did something kill the dinosaurs over a long period of time? Researchers studied the evidence, trying to figure out what had happened.

Now, most scientists think they have the answer. They believe that a large *asteroid* (a rocky object from space) struck Earth about 65 million years ago. This giant asteroid slammed into the Gulf of Mexico, creating a crater about 25 miles (40 kilometers) deep and 125 miles (200 kilometers) wide. The force of the impact blew down the trees in all the forests that covered North America. It caused a powerful earthquake and a huge *tsunami* (series of ocean waves) that covered the land as far north as southern Illinois.

Most importantly, the impact sent tons of rocky material into the sky, blocking the sunlight. For years after the event, the sky was dark over all of the Earth. Plants could not get the sunlight they needed to grow, and they died off. The animals that depended on the plants for food—and other animals that depended on the plant-eaters for food—died off as well, including most of the dinosaurs. We know that people had nothing to do with the dinosaurs becoming extinct. There were no people around at the time these animals lived. But other kinds of animals have become extinct in just the past few hundreds of years, and people certainly did have something to do with those extinctions.

# Steller's sea cow

In the cold waters around islands off the coast of Siberia, there once lived a giant animal. This animal was about 25 feet (8 meters) long and may have weighed as much as 10 tons (9 metric tons)—bigger and heavier than an African elephant! It looked somewhat like a huge seal. In fact, it was a relative of the seal. The skin on its big body was black, thick, and tough. This harmless creature lived in shallow water and spent most of its time eating seaweed. The sailors who first saw it called it a "sea cow."

Sea cows were discovered in 1741 by Russian sailors. Their ship was damaged in a storm, and they became stranded on an island near which the animals lived. The sailors survived by eating the meat of sea cows while they fixed their ship. Among them was a scientist named Georg Steller, who wrote about the animals. That is why they came to be called Steller's sea cows.

A few years later, fur hunters started coming to the islands to hunt seals and sea otters. They also hunted the sea cows for food. Even then, there were only about 2,000 sea cows. They lived near the shore, in small herds. This made them easy to hunt. Less than 30 years after sea cows were discovered, the hunters had killed them all. This giant, gentle animal had joined a growing list of extinct animals.

An artist who lived in the 1700's produced this drawing of the extinct dodo bird. He based the drawing on travelers' descriptions and earlier paintings.

The Dodo

Geo Edwards, Sculp: A.

# The dodo

ave you ever read the book *Alice in Wonderland?* If you have, you've met the dodo. It's the fat, funny bird that Alice talks to after she climbs out of the pool of tears.

There really were birds called dodos, but they couldn't talk, of course. They lived on a little island in the Indian Ocean, not far from Africa. They were large, chubby birds, a little bigger than a big turkey. Their stubby wings were too small for flying, and their legs were too short for running. So they waddled wherever they went.

No people lived on the island. No one even knew about it until the year 1507. Then, ships began to stop there for water and food. Sailors who went ashore to hunt had no trouble capturing the clumsy dodos. Dozens and dozens of the big birds were taken aboard ships and used for food.

People began living on the island in the 1600's. They, too, ate dodo birds. So did the dogs and pigs that people brought to the island. The dodos were easy to find and catch. They had no way of hiding or protecting themselves.

By 1681, there were no dodos left anywhere on the island. They had all been killed. The dodo was gone—forever.

# The blue buck

The blue buck was a beautiful animal, with glossy, bluish-brown fur. It lived in a small valley in South Africa.

People had lived there for hundreds of years. They hunted blue bucks and other animals. But with spears, and bows and arrows, they couldn't kill too many. Then, in the 1650's, people from Europe began to make South Africa their home. They had guns, and they rode horses, which made hunting easy.

South Africa was full of animals. The Europeans began to hunt many of them for their meat, for their skins, and for sport. Thousands of animals were killed each year. Many of these were blue bucks.

There weren't as many blue bucks as there were other kinds of animals, but the hunters did not care. They went on killing them. Each year there were fewer and fewer blue bucks. Still the killing went on. In the year 1800, the last one was shot. The blue buck was extinct.

An artist of the early
1800's captured the
beauty of passenger
pigeons in a water color.

# The passenger pigeon

When early explorers and European settlers first reached North America, many of them wrote about the vast numbers of a small, gray bird called the passenger pigeon. In the early 1600's, about 3 billion to 5 billion passenger pigeons lived mainly in an area stretching from the Great Lakes to the present state of New York. When the birds flew south for the winter, their flocks were so huge that they darkened the skies for several days as they passed overhead.

Passenger pigeons were about 15 to 16 inches (38 to 41 centimeters) long. Their gray heads and bodies were marked by shiny patches of pink, green, and purple. Passenger pigeons were similar to mourning doves, but mourning doves are smaller, and their markings are not as bright.

Passenger pigeons lived in the forests that once covered most of the eastern United States. They liked to live in large flocks and built their nests crowded together in the branches of trees. Often, the branches broke under the weight of all the nests.

As farmers began to chop down the trees to make way for fields, the birds' food supply dwindled. They began to eat the grain in the fields. Farmers shot the birds to protect their crops. In the 1800's, hunters began killing the birds to sell them for food in markets. In Petoskey, Michigan, near one of the last large nesting sites, hunters killed an estimated 50,000 birds a day for nearly 5 months. By the time laws were passed to stop the killing, it was too late.

In the early 1900's, no more passenger pigeons could be found in the wild. The last known passenger pigeon—a bird named Martha in honor of Martha Washington—died in 1914 at the Cincinnati Zoological Garden.

**12%**
**Birds**

**34%**
**Invertebrates**

**30%**
**Amphibians**

The number below each photo shows what percentage of the species in each category was threatened in 2010, according to the IUCN Red List.

# More and More

No one really knows how many *species* of plants and animals have become extinct, because no one knows how many species there were to begin with. (Species are groups of plants and animals that have characteristics in common; a male and female of the same species will have babies that are also of that species.) Scientists have been trying to count the number of species for years. But they are still not sure how many species there are.

By 2010, scientists had identified 1.9 million species. Many scientists think there are from 10 million to 20 million species in all. Some scientists think there may be as many as 100 million species.

Of the 1.9 million species that have been identified, scientists have counted or estimated the number of animals and plants left in about 48,000 of them. Of these, the scientists learned that, as of 2010, more than 17,000 species were threatened with extinction—more than one-third of all the species identified!

When scientists say that a species is "threatened," they mean something very specific. Scientists with the International

---

21% **Mammals**  28% **Reptiles**  32% **Fish**

Union for Conservation of Nature and Natural Resources (IUCN) have created a document called the Red List that shows how various species are doing. After a species has been identified, scientists classify it in one of the following categories: least concern, near threatened, vulnerable, endangered, critically endangered, extinct in the wild, and extinct.

Scientists have agreed on what these terms mean. "Extinct" means that no members of a species exist any more. "Extinct in the wild" means that the only members of a species left live in zoos or nature reserves. If a species is called "threatened," that means it was classified as either "vulnerable," "endangered," or "critically endangered," depending on how many plants or animals are left in the species or how safe their *habitat* is. (A habitat is the place where a species lives.) Species that are either "near threatened" or "least concern" are in the least danger.

Many people are doing what they can to prevent more species from becoming extinct and to reintroduce species found only in captivity back to the wild. But for many reasons, species are still disappearing; for example, hunting, pollution, climate change, and destruction of habitat. People are responsible for some of these factors. And people are the only ones who can fix the damage that has been done.

Scientists in
Churchill, Canada,
weigh a polar bear.

# Keeping Track

verywhere in the world there are people who study animals. Scientists, naturalists, conservationists, and other interested people often spend years watching certain kinds of animals. They keep careful records of the things they see and learn—and one of the things they keep track of is how many animals there are.

A mother bear wears a collar that sends out radio signals so that scientists can track her movements.

These people know that many kinds of animals are vanishing. Where they once saw thousands of animals, now there are only hundreds—sometimes only dozens. It is clear that these animals are in danger.

The smart, lively chimpanzee; the white-furred polar bear; the sleek and swift wild horse; the clever giant otter; the proud, prowling tiger—all these and many, many other creatures may soon be gone forever. Like the quagga, the sea cow, the dodo, the blue buck, and the passenger pigeon, they will become extinct—unless we do something now.

# Vanishing Animals Today

*"Over increasingly large areas of the United States, spring now comes unheralded by the return of the birds, and the early mornings are strangely silent where once they were filled with the beauty of bird song."*

**Rachel Carson**

Carson was an American marine biologist and science writer of the mid-1900's. Her book *Silent Spring* was the first to make people aware of the dangers of *pesticides* (poisons that kill weeds, insects, and other pests).

# The Empty Woods

The late afternoon sun hung low and red in the sky. It sent long shadows slanting through the woods. The leaves of the trees were just changing into their fall colors. Where the sunlight touched them, they glowed red, purple, and gold.

A narrow, dirt path wound in and out among the trees, and three people were walking along it. One was a tall, pleasant-faced woman with gray hair. The other two were a boy and girl.

From time to time, a soft breeze blew through the woods. Then the leaves of the trees would shiver with a rustling whisper. Except for this sound, and the buzz of insects, the forest was silent and peaceful. But from nearby there came the roar of cars and trucks on a big highway.

The woman and children rounded a turn in the path and came to a great, twisted, old oak tree. Down at the bottom of its gray trunk, where the tree's knobby roots clutched the earth, there was an opening. It looked like the entrance to a tiny cave. Seeing this, the little girl scampered to the tree. She knelt down to peer into the hollow trunk. Moments later, she looked up at the woman, disappointment on her face.

"I thought maybe a little animal lived here, Grandma," she announced. "But there's just some wet leaves and a rusty old can."

The woman smiled, a bit sadly. "I'm afraid there aren't very many animals left in these woods, Susie," she said. "A few birds and squirrels are about all. There were lots of different kinds of animals here when I was a little girl, though."

"What kinds of animals?" questioned the boy.

"Well, there were deer, Georgie," replied his grandmother. "A small herd of deer. They were very shy, but I'd see them once in a while. And I would often see their hoof marks in the dirt."

"Where are they now?" George asked.

The woman gave a sad shake of her head. "I guess they went somewhere else. The forest is just too small for them now. It used to be much bigger, but most of it was cleared away and houses were built on the land."

"What other animals were there?" Susie wanted to know.

"Lots of frogs," her grandmother told her. "I haven't seen a frog here for years now, but there used to be thousands of them. Especially the tiny ones called spring peepers. In the evenings, in springtime, the woods were filled with the sound they made—like soft little bells ringing. *Ching-ching-ching-ching.*"

"I know what a frog's like," Susie announced, bouncing on her toes with excitement. "There's a picture in my book. They're fat and green and bumpy, and they have great big mouths!"

Grandmother smiled. "I think that must be a picture of a bullfrog," she said. "They are bigger and fatter than the spring peepers. Bullfrogs make a sound like this"—she lowered her voice as much as she could—*"CHUGGERUM!"* The children laughed.

They had come to a tiny, slow-moving stream, crossed by a little stone bridge. Grandmother paused, looking down at the muddy bank and the still, brownish-colored water. Under the bridge, a broad patch of whitish scum floated on the surface of the water.

"Here is where most of the frogs used to live," said Grandmother. "I guess the water is too dirty for them now."

She pointed at a part of the bank not far from where they stood. "Right there, Susie, when I was just about your age, I found a big mud turtle lying on its back. The poor thing was waving its legs, trying to roll over. I turned him over and he crawled into the water and swam away. There were lots of turtles, but I'm afraid most of them were killed by cars after the big highway was built. They would wander out onto the road and get run over."

She sighed. "Thinking about it makes me sad. I miss them—the deer and the frogs and the turtles and all the other little creatures that are gone now."

"I miss them, too," the little girl declared.

George looked at her, scornfully. "How can you miss 'em? You never even saw 'em."

"I don't care!" she answered. "I *do* miss them! I wish they were still here so I could see them. It isn't fair!"

George looked at her for a moment. Then he looked down at the bank. He tried to imagine a fat mud turtle lying on its back, waving its legs. He saw himself scrambling down the bank to help it. He tried to imagine the footprints of the deer. He tried to hear the soft *ching-ching-ching* of the spring peepers.

But he couldn't. Those things were gone. He would never see or hear them. Suddenly, he felt cheated.

"You're right!" he said, scowling. "It isn't fair!"

# Vanishing Animals of
## Africa

These symbols will tell you whether the IUCN has classified an animal as vulnerable, endangered, or critically endangered.

⚠ Vulnerable

⚠ Endangered

⚠ Critically endangered

⚠ **The chimpanzee**

The first, faint light of dawn crept into the sky, pushing out night's darkness. One by one, the stars faded. Morning had come to the African rain forest.

High in a tree, a chimpanzee woke up. He had spent the night sleeping in a nest made of bent and twisted branches. He lazily yawned and scratched himself for several minutes. Then he climbed down from the tree and started out to find his morning meal.

Most of the time, the chimpanzee walked on all fours, his body bent forward, the knuckles of his hands touching the ground. When he stood to look around, he was about 5 feet (1.5 meters) tall.

In a few minutes, the chimpanzee found a tree that seemed to promise breakfast. He hurried into its branches. Sure enough, there were plenty of tasty leaf buds for a hungry chimp.

He munched contentedly. Suddenly, from a nearby part of the forest came a loud uproar—barking, chattering, screaming, and hooting! The chimpanzee stared in the direction of the sound. The hair on his body stood up with excitement. He leaped down from the tree and hurried toward the noise.

The clamor came from a clump of fig trees. There, more than a dozen chimpanzees scrambled about in the branches. The trees were full of ripe, juicy fruit, and the chimps were wild with excitement. Here was a feast!

The chimpanzee on the ground greeted the ones in the trees with hooting noises. He knew them all, because he traveled through the forest with them. They hooted greetings back at him.

He leaped into the tree. Before hurrying to find a good feeding place, he stopped, put his hand on the back of another male chimpanzee, and gave him a few scratches. He was showing his respect for the leader of the group.

For most of the morning, the band of chimpanzees stayed in the fig trees, eating their fill. As the sun rose high in the sky, the forest grew hot. Except for the steady whirr of insects, there was silence. The chimpanzees dozed in the shade of leafy branches, or sat scratching in each other's fur. Young chimps, two or three years old, chased each other wildly back and forth through the vines and branches.

By late afternoon, the forest was cool. The chimpanzees trooped off in search of a new feeding place. As the sun set, the forest filled with shadows. The chimps began to make sleeping nests in the nearest trees. Each animal, except for the very young ones, made its own nest and slept by itself. Mothers and babies curled up together in the mother's nest.

Night came to the forest. In their leafy tree beds, the chimpanzees slept, untroubled by anything.

But the chimpanzees of Africa are in trouble, even though they do not know it. In some parts of Africa, these creatures—so much like humans in so many ways—are being hunted by people for food or captured to be kept as pets. In other places, the forests where they live are being cut and burned to make room for houses and farms. Chimpanzees are also becoming sick and dying from diseases spread by human beings. Some scientists fear that in a short time, these wonderful creatures may be gone from the wild forever.

# ⚠ The indri

The indri is somewhat like a monkey with a dog's face. It lives high in the treetops in a small part of a hot, wet, mountainside forest.

Soon after sunrise each day, the forest fills with loud howling that means the indri is awake. During the morning, little groups of three, four, or five of these creatures move about together in the trees, feeding on leaves. Sometimes they sit on branches and sunbathe, stretching their arms above their heads as if they were worshiping the sun. In the hot after-noon hours, they sleep. But in the evening, they are noisy and active again.

When an indri comes down from the trees and walks on the ground, it looks like a little furry person. It hops along on its legs, with its body swaying and its arms spread out for balance, like a tightrope walk-er. When it stands upright this way, it is about 2 feet (0.6 meter) tall.

The indri is timid and peaceful. It eats leaves, fruits, and flowers, and it tries to hide from people. But it is in bad trouble. People hunt the indri for its meat. Also, its forest home is slowly being cut down—huge areas are gone already. The indri has nowhere else to go, for it can find food only in the place where it now lives.

# ⚠ The geometric tortoise

A tortoise is a turtle that lives on land. The geometric tortoise is a kind of tortoise with a beautiful black-and-yellow patterned shell. It is one of the rarest tortoises in the world and lives only in the Western Cape province of South Africa.

The geometric tortoise is not very big. Even when it is fully grown, its shell is only up to 5 or 6 inches (13 or 15 centimeters) wide. The patterns on the shell look like the bright yellow rays of the sun on a black background. The patterns and colors help the tortoise blend in with its surroundings so that *predators* (animals that kill other animals and eat them for food) cannot see it.

The area in which the geometric tortoise lives in South Africa was once a tropical rain forest. But millions of years ago, the region became drier, and trees are now rare there. Today, the area is filled with evergreen shrubs, grasses, and many types of flowering plants. Geometric tortoises hide in the undergrowth from predators and to escape the heat. They feed on the leaves, flowers, and grass.

In the spring, female geometric tortoises dig a hole in the ground and lay their eggs in it. They cover the hole with grasses. When the baby tortoises hatch, they dig their way out of the hole.

Even though they have a strong shell, geometric tortoises face many dangers. Baboons, ostriches, crows, storks, and many other kinds of birds and animals eat them. People eat their eggs, too, and make decorations out of their beautiful shells. And uncontrolled wildfires often sweep through their habitat, moving much more quickly than the tortoises can run to escape them.

A scientist first described the geometric tortoise in 1758. In 1969, when conservationists could not find any more of the tortoises, they thought the animal was already extinct. But in 1972, a scientist discovered a small number of geometric tortoises in several places in Western Cape province. Private and governmental nature reserves were set up in the province to keep the tortoise safe. Today, scientists think there may only be a couple thousand geometric tortoises left.

# ⚠ The African wild dog

As dawn lights up the sky of South Africa, a wild dog pack gets ready for the morning hunt. The dogs touch their noses together. They jump playfully at each other, wagging their tails. Then, off they go. One dog stays behind to guard the pups that are hidden in the den.

There are usually from 10 to 20 dogs in a pack. They hunt by spreading out in a long line. Silently, they trot across the vast yellow plain.

The dogs move toward a herd of wildebeests. When the wildebeests see the dogs, they take to their heels. The dogs streak after them, yipping with excitement. The hunt is on!

One wildebeest soon becomes tired and slows down. The dogs quickly close in on it. Some of them cut in front of it, separating it from the rest of the herd. Surrounded and exhausted, the wildebeest stops. The dogs swarm over it and pull it down.

They are soon feasting on the wildebeest's flesh. As they eat, they never snarl or snap at each other as tame dogs often do. The wild dogs of Africa get along very well and share almost everything with one another.

When the dogs have eaten all they can hold, they hurry back to the den. There they spit out chunks of meat for the guard dog and the pups.

The wild dogs do an important job. They help keep things in balance by holding down the numbers of many kinds of animals. But the wild dogs are in danger. Many people dislike them. The dogs used to live throughout much of Africa. Now only a few thousand are left, in southern and eastern Africa. They have been hunted and poisoned, and settlers have gradually taken over areas where the dogs used to roam.

⚠ **The lowland gorilla**

**Y**ou probably shiver at the thought of meeting a big, shaggy, fierce-looking wild gorilla. A full-grown gorilla may stand 6 feet (1.8 meters) tall and weigh 390 pounds (177 kilograms). It could easily crush you.

But gorillas are really very gentle and peaceful. Several scientists, both men and women, have lived close to groups of wild gorillas—and made friends with them!

These big, shaggy creatures live in forests. They travel about in groups in search of food. They eat leaves, bark, fruits, flowers, and the tender shoots of plants. They seldom eat meat, or drink water—they get all the water they need from the juicy plants they eat.

Gorillas spend their days eating and sleeping. While grown-ups take naps, the young gorillas play and wrestle and chase one another, just as children do. At night, each grown-up makes itself a nest of vines and branches to sleep in. Mothers and babies sleep together.

Gorillas are four-footed animals. They walk on their feet and the knuckles of their hands. Although they sometimes climb trees, they never swing through the trees, as some people believe. They are mainly ground animals.

There are three kinds of gorillas: western lowland gorillas, eastern lowland gorillas, and mountain gorillas. All three kinds are in trouble, but the western lowland gorillas, who live in west central Africa, face the greatest danger. People are taking over their lands for farming, logging, and mining. They are killing the gorillas and selling them as "bushmeat." And the gorillas are dying of diseases spread by humans.

⚠ **The northern bald ibis**

The northern bald ibis is not a very pretty bird. It has a red face, a bald forehead, and a strange tuft of long, narrow feathers at the back of its head. It is a medium-sized bird, about 28 to 32 inches (70 to 80 centimeters) long. Its body is covered in black feathers that become *iridescent* (changing colors) when the sun hits them, flashing purple, green, and copper.

The ancient Egyptians revered the northern bald ibis. They carved its image on the walls of their tombs and even invented a *hieroglyph* (a picture or symbol that represented a sound, word, or idea) for the bird.

Northern bald ibises are mostly quiet birds. They live in groups called colonies, but the only sounds they make are hisses and grunts when they are sitting on their nest or when the males are trying to attract a female. The birds nest in rocky areas, atop cliffs or among boulders. They build a loose nest of small branches and line it with whatever soft materials they can find. They eat berries and plant shoots and practically any kind of animal—either alive or dead—including insects, scorpions, worms, snails, fish, snakes, and even smaller birds.

At one time, the northern bald ibis lived in parts of central and southern Europe, North Africa, and the Middle East. But it disappeared from Europe in the 1500's. Researchers think that people moved onto lands that served as its habitat. About a dozen of the birds were discovered in Syria, in the Middle East, in 2002. By 2009, only a handful remained. The rest were shot by hunters or died after eating food poisoned with DDT (a pesticide). Now, only a few remain in Syria. The only place left with a sizable colony of northern bald ibises is Morocco, in North Africa, where about 500 of the birds live. A national park was established in Morocco to protect the birds' nesting site, and local people are helping scientists care for the birds.

# ⚠ The black rhinoceros

bright, full moon hangs in the night sky. Its cool light turns the African plain into a silvery sea of grass. Here and there stand shadowy clusters of trees and bushes.

A huge, bulky gray beast is feeding on the grass. The moonlight gleams on the two horns that stick up from its nose. It is a male black rhinoceros, standing about 5 feet (1.5 meters) high at the shoulders and about 12 feet (3.6 meters) long. This great animal weighs about 1.5 tons (1.4 metric tons).

All night long the big animal eats, for it takes a lot of grass to fill that great body. As he stands chewing, his tubelike ears twitch and turn in every direction, listening for the slightest sound. The rhino cannot see very well, but his keen senses of hearing and smell tell him what is happening around him.

By midmorning, the plain begins to grow hot under the fierce African sun. Big feet thudding on the earth, the rhino trots off across the plain. He may look clumsy because of his size and weight. But he can run as fast as a race horse for a short distance.

The rhino comes to a large, shallow pool of rain water. He dips his nose into the water and drinks for a long time. Then he flops down to wallow in the mud. He rolls around, smearing himself thickly with mud, and then goes to sleep.

Under the hot sun, the mud dries into a hard, dark crust. That may be where the name "black rhinoceros" came from. The crust protects the rhino's body from the bites of flies and insects.

For millions of years rhinos have lived this kind of life—eating, sleeping, and wallowing in their muddy pools or in piles of dust. Once, there were rhinos in most parts of the world, even in Europe and North America. Today, there are much fewer rhinos—and only in parts of Africa and Asia. Of the two kinds that live in Africa, the black rhinos are in the most danger. For many years they have been hunted for their horns, which some people believe have magic powers. Today, the black rhinoceros is critically endangered. In Asia, two kinds of rhinoceros—the Javan and the Sumatran—are critically endangered as well.

## ⚠ The addax

The home of the addax is the barren, sandy wastes of the Sahara. Here, small herds, led by an old male, travel about searching for tough desert grass to eat. An addax can live in parts of the desert where not even a camel can stay alive. In fact, an addax can go for weeks, and even months, without taking a drink of water! It gets all the water it needs from the plants it eats.

The addax is a member of the antelope family. In winter, its coat is grayish-brown, but its summer coat is milky white. An addax is about 3.5 feet (107 centimeters) high. Its graceful, curling horns are often more than a yard (meter) long. Its short tail seems to wiggle all the time.

Even though the addax can live in some of the harshest conditions in the world, it is not safe. Since the early 1900's, people have hunted the addax to near extinction for its meat. And its habitat has dwindled as farmers learned to grow crops at the edge of the desert. Only a few hundred addax still live in the Sahara—and they are still being hunted.

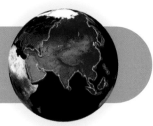

# ⚠ The Bengal tiger

olden eyes gleaming, the Bengal tiger prowled through the tall grass of the meadow. It was near sundown, and the grass glowed deep orange in the light of the red, setting sun. With his orange-red body and black stripes, the tiger could hardly be seen as he moved through the shadow-filled grass.

Slowly, blackness filled the sky. This was the tiger's hunting time. He had not eaten for several days and was ready for a hearty meal.

Hours passed, and the tiger prowled on. Once, he met another tiger. The two big cats rubbed their heads together in greeting. Then each went on its way into the night in search of food.

Suddenly, the tiger stopped. He could see well in the darkness, and about a hundred yards ahead of him stood a herd of deer, calmly grazing.

The tiger pressed his body close to the ground and began to move again, sliding through the tall grass. The deer continued to munch mouthfuls of grass, unaware of any danger. Now the tiger was only 30 feet (9 meters) away.

The tiger stood up. Then, with a terrifying roar, he charged! His body—9 feet (3 meters) long and weighing 400 pounds (180 kilograms)—moved in one enormous leap and came smashing down on the back of a startled deer. As the deer fell to the ground, the tiger buried his teeth in its throat.

All night long the tiger ate, gobbling nearly 50 pounds (23 kilograms) of meat! When the sun came up, the tiger dragged the deer's body to a hiding place among some rocks. Then the big striped cat settled down to sleep. After his enormous meal, and with plenty of "leftovers," the tiger would not have to hunt again for several days.

In 1900, there were about 100,000 tigers of several different kinds living in Asia, from Turkey in the west to Russia in the east. But for many years, people hunted tigers for their heads, skins, teeth, and claws. Today, there are no more than about 5,000 tigers living in the wild. About half of these are Bengal tigers.

Also, as the human population grew and farms and villages appeared, the size of the tiger's hunting area became more than 40 percent smaller. In fact, by 2010, the conservation group World Wildlife Fund estimated that there were more tigers in captivity in the United States than there are left in the wild.

# ⚠ The orangutan

Orangutans seem to be the world's sleepiest animals! They go to bed before it's dark. They get up late in the morning. And they spend most of the day taking naps!

These long-armed, red-furred apes live in warm, wet forests. One kind lives on the island of Borneo, and the other kind lives on the island of Sumatra.

Long ago, the people who lived on the islands believed that the apes were just a different kind of people who wanted to live in the woods. That's why the people named them *orangutan,* which means "man of the woods."

Orangutans aren't as big as their cousins, the gorillas and chimpanzees. A full-grown male orang is usually only about 4 feet (1.2 meters) tall. And orangutans don't spend most of the time on the ground as chimps and gorillas do—they live in the trees. Orangutans move about in search of fruit, their main food. They also eat leaves, insects, and bark. At night, they make nests of branches to sleep in. They often build a little "roof" over a nest to keep rain out.

Orangutans are endangered for several reasons. Lumber companies are rapidly cutting down the forests where they live. Plantations and roads are replacing their forest habitat. Also, people hunt the orangs. The hunters kill the mothers and take the babies to sell as pets or to zoos. On Borneo, many orangs are also killed in fires. During some years, there is little rainfall, and the forests dry out and burn.

There are probably fewer than 7,000 orangutans left in Sumatra. Scientists found more orangs in Borneo in the early 2000's but, since then, many more forests have disappeared. How long will it be before the orangs disappear, too?

# ⚠ The snow leopard

ost people think of leopards as being large, black-spotted, orange cats. But a snow leopard has smoky-gray fur with black spots shaped like rings. And most people think of leopards as living in hot forests. But snow leopards live high in the cold, rocky mountains of central Asia, where patches of white snow lie among the brown boulders.

A snow leopard isn't as big as a lion or a tiger, but it's still a very big cat. A full-grown snow leopard is often about 4 feet (1.3 meters) long (without its long, fluffy tail). It may weigh as much as 120 pounds (54 kilograms).

A snow leopard likes to live by itself. Each snow leopard has its own den. Usually this is just a shallow cave where the leopard sleeps. The leopards hunt by themselves, too. They search for wild goats and other animals that live in the mountains. They creep in close to a herd and leap onto one of the animals from a boulder. A snow leopard usually feeds for several days on an animal it has killed.

Snow leopards are sometimes shot by farmers because the leopards attack the farmers' herds of tame sheep and goats. But the snow leopard is mostly in trouble just because it is beautiful—hunters can get a lot of money for its silky, smoky fur. By the early 2000's, fewer than 6,500 of these striking animals remained.

# ⚠ The Komodo dragon

The dragon was hungry. For several hours it had been hiding beside a trail used by deer coming down from the mountain. The dragon waited, hidden beneath a fallen tree. Its forked tongue darted in and out.

There was a sound of hoofs on the trail. Three deer appeared, moving along one after the other.

They had been feeding on grass high up on the hot, sunny mountainside. Now, they wanted to find a cool, shady place in the forest where they could sleep.

Suddenly, the huge, scaly dragon lunged out at the first deer! Sharp, savage teeth sank into one of the deer's thin legs. The deer kicked and struggled in panic, trying to free itself. Its companions raced away in terror.

The deer fell to the ground. Instantly, the dragon killed it. Then the big, scaly monster began to feed, gulping down huge chucks of deer—hide, hair, bones, and all!

The dragon is not a real dragon, of course. But it looks a lot like a dragon. It is called a Komodo dragon because it lives on the island of Komodo, as well as four other small islands, in Indonesia.

The Komodo dragon is the largest of all lizards and one of the biggest of all reptiles. Komodo dragons may grow to be as much as 10 feet (3 meters) long. They may weigh up to 365 pounds (165 kilograms). With their sharp teeth and claws, they are fierce hunters. A full-grown Komodo dragon can even attack and kill a big water buffalo!

Komodo dragons have become endangered because people have destroyed their habitat and over-hunted their prey. People also trapped the dragons to sell them as pets and killed them for their body parts. Today, there may be only about 2,500 Komodo drag-ons left. Even more worrisome is the fact that only about one-fourth of the remaining dragons are females. That means that there may not be enough baby Komodo dragons born for the species to survive.

# ⚠ The wild horse

**W**hen most of us think of "wild" horses, we think of the western United States, where some horses still roam free. But those horses are not really wild. They are the descendants of *domestic* (tame) horses that ran away.

The only true wild horses left in the world live in Asia, in the countries of Mongolia and China. They are called Przewalski's *(puhr zheh VAHL skihz)* horses after the Russian explorer who first identified them in 1881.

Przewalski's horses actually became extinct in the wild by the 1960's. But about a dozen of them had been kept safe on reserves. Conservationists used this small herd to breed more wild horses in captivity. Since the 1990's, about 200 of these horses have been reintroduced to the *steppes* (vast, treeless plains) of Mongolia. In 2007, a smaller group was reintroduced in China. Today, there are about 300 wild horses in Asia.

Przewalski's horse is related to the domestic horse, but it looks more like a donkey. It has a grayish-brown coat, a brown mane, and a dark stripe down its back. Its mane is short and stands straight up, unlike the flowing mane of a domestic horse.

Conservationists are thrilled that Przewalski's horses once again roam free on the steppes of Asia. But they are still very concerned about how long the species will last. As the wild horses come into contact with domestic horses, there is a danger of their breeding with domestic horses and losing their unique *genes*. (Genes are the parts of cells that carry the characteristics that parents pass on to their offspring.) In addition, wolves often attack and kill the young foals. Also, people are intruding on the horses' habitat, letting their livestock feed until the land is overgrazed and the watering holes are used up. It will take a lot of effort over a long time to keep Przewalski's horses safe in the wild.

# ⚠ The Ganges dolphin

**W**hen most people think of dolphins, they think of animals that live in the oceans. But there are actually two kinds of dolphins. Dolphins that live in salt water are called marine dolphins. Dolphins that live in fresh or slightly salty water are called river dolphins. River dolphins look a little different than marine dolphins. They live in rivers and lakes in Asia and South America instead of in the world's oceans. The Ganges dolphin—also called the South Asian river dolphin—is a river dolphin.

The Ganges dolphin lives only in freshwater rivers in northern India, Nepal, and Bangladesh. It has a gray body, which can be up to 8 feet (2.5 meters) long, and it can weigh as much as 190 pounds (85 kilograms). The females are usually longer and heavier than the males. The Ganges dolphin has a long snout that widens at the tip and a low, triangular fin on its back. It has small eyes and is nearly blind because its eyes have no *lenses* (one of the parts of the *eye* that helps it to focus). Ganges dolphins feed mostly on fish.

Ganges dolphins, like other types of river dolphins, are endangered. Scientists think there may only be about 2,000 to 4,000 Ganges dolphins left. They are disappearing for several reasons. As the countries of Asia become more industrialized, their rivers are becoming more polluted. The polluted water is bad for the fish the dolphins eat and for the dolphins themselves. In addition, as dams are built across rivers to provide energy for industry, they cause the dolphins to be divided into small, isolated groups and leave them smaller areas in which to feed.

Hunters are also taking their toll. Some tribal people hunt dolphins for food. Dolphins also drown in nets that fishing crews set out to catch fish.

In 2010, the government of India named the Ganges river dolphin its national aquatic animal. Government officials hoped that such a move would help to keep these gentle creatures safe.

# ⚠ The giant panda

The giant panda is one of the most loved animals in the world. It has a chubby white body with black legs, a wide band of black across the shoulders, and a short tail, which is usually white. It also has a large, round white head, with small black ears and black patches around its eyes. The giant panda can grow to about 5 to 6 feet (1.5 to 1.8 meters) tall and can weigh as much as 200 to 300 pounds (90 to 140 kilograms).

Giant pandas are members of the bear family. Their bodies are shaped like a bear's, and, like bears, giant pandas can stand on their hind legs. (Another kind of panda—called the red panda—is much smaller than the giant panda and does not belong to the bear family; it looks and acts more like a raccoon.)

Giant pandas live in the wild in only one place in the world—central China. There, they live in bamboo forests on mountain slopes. In fact, the bamboo plant is almost the only food that giant pandas eat. And, because the animals are so big, they eat a lot of bamboo—85 pounds (39 kilograms) per day, in some cases. Giant pandas spend a large part of their day sitting around, eating the shoots, stems, and leaves of bamboo.

Most of the time, giant pandas live by themselves. But cubs live with their mothers for about two years, and adult giant pandas get together to *mate* (produce offspring) from March through May of each year.

Although conservationists have been working to save the giant panda from becoming extinct since the 1960's, the species remains endangered. There are about 1,500 to 2,000 giant pandas left in the wild. About 250 other giant pandas live on reserves in China or in zoos throughout the world. The main threat to the giant panda is the loss of its habitat and its bamboo food supply. Many of the forests in which the giant panda lived were cut down for wood or to make way for farmland. And in places where bamboo still grows, the plants die off in regular cycles, endangering the giant pandas that live there.

The Chinese government is taking steps to protect both the giant pandas and the areas in which they live. Zoos in various countries have been helping, too. Under an agreement with China, zoos accept pairs of adult pandas on temporary loan. Scientists at the zoos study the breeding and conservation of pandas, and any babies born to the pairs are returned to China when they are old enough to live on their own. Of course, in the meantime, people throughout the world flock to the zoos to enjoy each of the rare giant panda cubs that is born.

# ⚠ The Asian elephant

D o you know how to tell an Asian elephant from an African elephant? You can tell them apart by the size of their ears. An African elephant has big, floppy ears that look like fans. An Asian elephant's ears are much smaller.

The Asian elephant—also known as the Indian elephant—lives on the mainland of southeast Asia and on the islands of Sri Lanka, Borneo, and Sumatra. Asian elephants live mainly in thick, green forests and jungles. They spend most of their time just eating—leaves, grass, vines, the tender shoots of plants, and fruits. They love to wallow in mud holes and bathe in streams. Asian elephants can live to be 60 to 70 years old.

A grown-up male Asian elephant is about 9 to 10.5 feet (2.7 to 3.2 meters) tall. The older male elephants live by themselves. The females live in herds, with their little ones and sometimes with a few young males. There are usually from 10 to 50 elephants in a herd, and the leader is usually the oldest female in the herd.

Once there were hundreds of thousands of wild Asian elephants. Today, there may be between 30,000 and 40,000 left. Most of the forests where they once roamed have been cut down. The few parts of forest that are left have been turned into national parks, but the parks are not really big enough for the elephants. These animals need lots of room in order to find food. So, in their search for food, the elephants sometimes leave the forests and cause damage to nearby farms. Unless the Asian elephants can be given more room and better protection, they may soon be gone from the wild.

⚠ **The Tasmanian devil**

Stars twinkle and a bright full moon glows above the Australian island of Tasmania. But in the forest, it is dark and still. A small, spotted, cat-like creature called a quoll feasts contentedly on a *carcass* (dead body of an animal) that it has discovered on the forest floor.

Suddenly, a spine-chilling shriek pierces the night. The quoll looks up to see a fierce, medium-sized creature approaching on short, stubby legs. The animal has jet-black fur with striking white markings. Its ears seem to glow bright red, and its mouth is stretched wide in a snarl over large, white teeth in a massive head. The sound it is making is enough to "raise the devil," as the early Australian settlers used to say.

The quoll doesn't think twice. It turns and disappears into the undergrowth as quickly as its legs can carry it. The Tasmanian devil, as the newly arrived creature is called, settles in to enjoy the prize it has stolen, cracking the skull of the carcass easily with its bone-crushing jaws.

Soon, other Tasmanian devils gather at the scene. The female who stole the carcass from the quoll growls and screams at them but allows them to eat. When she has had her fill, she makes her way back over several miles of forest paths to a hollow log where she has made her den. There, her four young await their mother's return. She carried them in a pouch, much like a kangaroo does, for about four months. Now, for the next nine months, they will depend on her milk before they begin to eat solid food. Then, the young will be on their own, eating and traveling about for miles by night and sleeping by day.

Tasmanian devils, which are found only on the island of Tasmania, have been a threatened species for a long time. Beginning in the mid-1800's, farmers often trapped and poisoned them because the devils attacked and killed livestock. Australia passed laws in 1941 forbidding the killing of Tasmanian devils.

In the 1990's, a different kind of disaster struck. Tasmanian devils began to sicken and die from a cancer scientists call devil facial tumor disease. When devils fight and bite each other, they spread the disease.

By 2010, about 70 percent of all wild Tasmanian devils had died of the highly infectious cancer. Some scientists thought that a virus might cause the illness. If so, researchers may one day develop a vaccine that would prevent the disease. But will they develop one in time to save the devils?

# ⚠ The numbat

**T**he numbat is a small creature that lives only in the southwestern corner of Western Australia. It grows to about 10 inches (25 centimeters) long. It has rusty-red fur with dramatic white stripes on its hind end and a fluffy tail that it carries straight up like a bristly brush. Its snout is pointy. Inside are 52 teeth of different shapes and sizes.

Numbats live in woodlands. They spend their days "snuffling" along the ground, looking for termites in dead trees, logs, and the leaf litter found on the forest floor. When a numbat finds a termite colony, it digs with its tiny front feet until it reaches the termites' underground tunnels. Then, it uses its long, sticky tongue—which can be half the length of its body—to pull out the termites. A numbat can eat more than 10,000 termites a day.

Female numbats usually have about four babies each year. When the babies are born, they are blind and hairless. They cling to their mother's belly fur for about six months. After that, the mother leaves them in a burrow while she goes out during the daytime to eat. The babies can live on their own when they are about 10 months old.

Numbats are an endangered species for several reasons. A long *drought* (time of little or no rainfall) in Australia during the late 1990's and 2000's caused frequent forest fires, which burned the logs where numbats live and bear their young. Also, the red fox, which did not originally live in Australia but was brought there by settlers, preys on numbats, killing significant numbers of them each year. Scientists have introduced a program to control the red fox population. They have also started several colonies of numbats in captivity. They hope to raise enough of the creatures to reintroduce them into the wild.

# ⚠ The hairy-nosed wombat

ome people think it looks like a beaver without a tail. Others say it looks like a badger. But it really doesn't look quite like either one. It looks like—well, a wombat. This pudgy, short-legged, snub-nosed creature is about 3 feet (0.9 meter) long. It has a tiny stump of a tail. And, like most other Australian mammals, a wombat has a pouch in which it carries its babies.

The hairy-nosed wombat is an expert digger. It lies on its side and digs with the strong, curved claws on all four of its feet. It likes to make long, long tunnels in soft soil beneath cliffs and boulders. At the end of the tunnel it makes a large nest of leaves and bark. There it sleeps during the day, coming out at night to eat grass and roots.

There are three kinds of wombats—the common wombat, the southern hairy-nosed wombat, and the northern hairy-nosed wombat. The first two kinds have large populations. But the northern hairy-nosed wombat, which lives on the plains of northern Australia, is critically endangered. People who settled Australia brought rabbits and livestock with them. Both of these animals eat the wombats' food. The rabbits also live in the wombats' burrows. By 2008, there were only about 100 northern hairy-nosed wombats left.

⚠ **The Gouldian finch**

The Gouldian finch is one of the most beautiful birds in Australia. People who have seen large flocks of the birds landing at a water hole to drink have described the experience as seeing a rainbow in flight. Unfortunately, such an experience has become quite rare, as the birds are disappearing.

Gouldian finches are small birds, about 5 to 5.5 inches (13 to 14 centimeters) long. They have an upper chest of light purple; a lower chest of yellow; green wings edged with brown; and blue and black tail feathers. The necks of Gouldian finches are black and their heads are outlined in turquoise blue. But the heads themselves can be any of three different colors—black, red, or yellow. Black-headed Gouldian finches are the most common, and yellow-headed ones are the most rare.

Gouldian finches live in northern Australia. Their habitats are called savannas, where there are open plains, water, and some trees. The finches make their nests in tree hollows. There, a female may lay four to eight eggs. Both the male and female sit on the eggs until they hatch. And both parents take care of the young until they are about three weeks old and ready to leave the nest.

Gouldian finches eat spiders and such insects as beetles, termites, and flies. But their favorite food is the seeds from certain grasses that grow in the savanna only during the wet season. This diet is the main reason the birds are endangered today. Drought and wildfires in Australia during the 2000's destroyed the trees the finches nest in and limited the growth of the grasses whose seeds they eat. Cattle, horses, and wild pigs have also eaten the grasses and trampled the area around water holes. Until the 1980's, many Gouldian finches were captured and sold as pets.

Conservationists have already taken steps to help Gouldian finches. They stopped the pet trade in the late 1980's, bought land to expand the finches' habitat, and set regulations for grazing cattle and managing wildfires. They hope that with these measures, we will be seeing "rainbows in flight" for many years to come.

# ⚠ The banded hare-wallaby

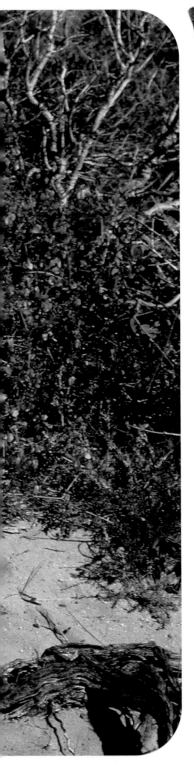

allabies are animals that look like little kangaroos. Female wallabies carry their babies—called joeys— in pouches the same way female kangaroos do.

There are several kinds of wallabies, ranging in size from 22 inches (55 centimeters) long to nearly 6 feet (1.8 meters) long, including the tail. The banded hare-wallaby is one of the smaller wallabies. It measures about 32 inches (81 centimeters) long. Its name comes from the fact that it has long gray fur with dark, horizontal stripes that begin at the middle of the back and end at the base of its long tail. It also resembles a *hare* (a relative of the rabbit).

Banded hare-wallabies have long, strong hind legs. They use them to hop from place to place while their tails help them to keep their balance. Some kinds of wallabies prefer to live alone. But banded hare-wallabies are very social. They build their nests in the same areas, under dense brush. They move about and look for food at night and sleep in their nests during the day.

Banded hare-wallabies do not eat meat. They eat grasses, fruit, and small plants.

Banded hare-wallabies once lived across the southwestern part of Australia. But they have not been seen on the mainland since about 1960. Today they are found only on Australia's Bernier and Dorre islands. They are endangered because such animals as cats and foxes—brought to the mainland by settlers—preyed on the banded hare-wallabies and also ate their food supply. Besides protecting the wallabies on the islands, scientists hope to save the banded hare-wallaby by reintroducing it to protected areas on the mainland.

⚠ **The wisent**

n a clearing deep inside an ancient forest, where some of the trees are 600 years old, two enormous shaggy beasts butt heads in a struggle for dominance. Both males, they stand 6 feet (1.8 meters) tall at the shoulders and weigh some 2,000 pounds (907 kilograms). They are brownish-black, with beards under their chins and short, sharp, curving horns on their heads. They look like buffalo, or American bison, only smaller. These animals are European bison, also known as wisent, and they represent a wonderful success story. Wisent became extinct in the wild after World War I (1914-1918), but conservationists brought them back.

Wisent once roamed throughout most of Europe, from England to northern Spain in the west and to Russia in the east. They lived in both thick, leafy woodlands and in grasslands, traveling in large herds and eating leaves, twigs, and tree bark. As the population of Europe grew and more and more people chopped down trees to build farms or to make their living by logging, the forests became smaller. The herds of wisent became smaller, too. People hunted them for their meat and hide and destroyed their food supply. By the early 1900's, the only wisent left in the wild lived in a woodland called Bialowieza Forest in northern Europe. There, what was thought to be the last wisent was killed in 1919.

Luckily, in the late 1800's, the Russian *czars* (rulers) who owned the forest at that time had sent pairs of wisent to zoos around the world as gifts. There, the wisent had been preserved, and more than 50 of them remained. In 1929, conservationists brought some of them back to Bialowieza Forest, where they established a herd in a protected area. In 1952, some of the descendants of these wisent were released to live wild in the forest again.

Today, Bialowieza Forest lies along the border of Poland and Belarus. Large parts of the forest have been declared national parks and are protected

from agriculture and logging. Tourists, escorted by guides, are allowed to visit parts of the forest and see the unique plants and animals that live there. Some species of animals are not found anywhere else in the world. The ancient oaks—with trunks that are as much as 275 inches (700 centimeters) around—make Bialowieza one of the oldest, most primitive forests in the world. Scientists estimate that more than 1,000 wisent now live wild in the forest, while nearly that many still remain in captive herds. With plans in place to manage both the forest and the animals, conservationists hope that wisent will never again be brought to the brink of extinction.

# ⚠ The Spanish lynx

The lynx is a cousin of the lion, tiger, leopard, and jaguar. But it is a cat with a special sort of look. Most cats have rounded ears and long tails. But a lynx's ears come to sharp points and have spikes of fur on the tips. And instead of being long, a lynx's tail is short and stubby. Thick whiskers hang from a lynx's cheeks. Its head looks too small for its 3-foot- (0.9-meter-) long body, and its feet seem much too big.

The Spanish lynx is a forest animal. It prowls among the trees, after dark, hunting mostly for rabbits though it will occasionally catch other small animals and birds as well. The lynx is a fast, fierce hunter that can climb trees easily and swim well. Its large, fluffy feet help it move quickly and easily over thick snow.

Spanish lynxes once lived almost everywhere in Spain and Portugal. But most of the forests where they lived have been cut down. And the rabbits that make up most of their food supply have been over-hunted. Today, only about 100 of these handsome cats are left in the few wild places left in Spain. By 2002, not a single Spanish lynx could be found in Portugal.

# ⚠ The Mediterranean monk seal

**M**ost seals are cold-water creatures that live in icy northern seas. But the small, dark-brown seals called monk seals like warm places. For many thousands of years they have lived in the warm waters of the Mediterranean, Adriatic, and Black seas. Small groups of monk seals often stay in rocky caves on islands and beaches.

The ancient·Greeks and Romans seem to have liked these seals. Greek and Roman poets wrote about them. The Greeks even put an image of the monk seal on some of their coins.

But this was long ago, when not many people lived in that part of the world. As time went by, there were more and more people. Many of these people fished for a living. And fishing is how the monk seals make *their* living, for they are fish-eaters.

Most fishermen soon felt there were too many monk seals eating too many fish. So the fishermen began to kill monk seals and kept on killing them for hundreds of years.

Today, there are fewer than 500 monk seals left, mostly on the coasts of Greece and western Turkey. Unless scientists can figure out how to help this creature, the Mediterranean monk seal will surely become extinct.

# ⚠ The European mink

inks are small, slender creatures that have been prized for hundreds of years for their luxurious winter fur. Their fur has been used to make such warm clothing as coats, jackets, stoles, and hats.

Minks live near fresh water, on the banks of rivers, streams, lakes, and marshes. They dive in and use their partly webbed feet to catch frogs, crayfish, and fish. Minks also hunt on land, where they may catch birds, mice, rabbits, snakes, and insects.

Minks live alone and are very protective of their hunting territory. A mink may make a home for itself among tree roots, dig a burrow, or take over the burrow of another small creature called a water vole. A female mink has from 2 to 7 babies— called kittens or kits—each year. The kits stay with their mother for about 11 weeks before they begin to catch their own food.

The European mink once lived throughout Europe. But because of overhunting and the destruction of their habitat, European minks are found today only in small, isolated groups in southwestern France, northern Spain, Belarus, Estonia, Romania, and Russia.

The biggest threat to European minks today is the American mink. American minks were brought to Europe in 1926 to establish commercial fur farms. American minks are a little larger than their European cousins, and they were more plentiful, so their fur became more commercially valuable. Over the years, many American minks escaped from the fur farms. And because they are bigger than European minks, they drove the European minks out of their burrows and hunting territories. American minks also *bred with* (had babies with) European minks, causing fewer pure European minks to be born.

Today, conservationists are trying to help European minks by moving them to islands in Europe that American minks cannot reach. There, they hope that the European minks will reproduce in large enough numbers to keep the species from dying out.

⚠ **The Dalmatian pelican**

he Dalmatian pelican is an unusual sight—it has yellow eyes, a curly crest on top of its head, and a long bill under which hangs a large pouch. The pouch turns dark red in early spring, when the bird is looking for a mate. Weighing nearly 30 pounds (14 kilograms), the Dalmatian pelican is one of the heaviest flying seabirds in the world. Its short legs and big body make it look a little clumsy on land. But it is a beautiful sight when it soars into the air on its huge, white wings.

Dalmatian pelicans are only one of seven different kinds of pelicans. There are pelicans on every continent except Antarctica. The Dalmatian pelican once lived across most of Europe. But now it is found mainly in isolated groups in several countries of eastern Europe, especially Kazakhstan and Greece.

In the springtime, male and female pelicans work together to build a nest on the ground. They carry twigs, grass, and feathers to the nest in their pouches. The female lays one or two eggs, but often raises only one chick, as the baby is called. Both parents take turns *incubating* the egg (keeping it warm). They hold it either on top of, or beneath, their webbed feet.

After the egg hatches, the parents bring food back to the nest for the chick. Dalmatian pelicans eat only fish. They scoop up the fish in their pouches, holding their bills open so that all the extra water can drain out.

When the chick is a few weeks old, it joins a large group, or pod, of other chicks. Somehow, pelican parents recognize their own chick among the group and will not feed any other chick.

The Dalmatian pelican has become vulnerable for several reasons. Its wetland habitat continues to be drained, to make way for farms or building sites. Each year, pelicans die because of water pollution and through collisions with overhead power lines. In addition, fishing crews kill pelicans because the birds eat a lot of fish, threatening their livelihoods.

Conservationists are currently taking steps to change some of these conditions. They are encouraging governments to bury power lines or make them more visible, to better manage wetlands, and to protect fish populations from overfishing, so that there is enough food for people and animals alike.

⚠ **The red wolf**

t was early spring. The winter snow had covered the land like a white blanket. But the snow had melted, and tiny new plants were pushing their pale green heads out of the damp, brown earth.

Six baby wolves peeped out at the world from the entrance of a den dug among the roots of a tall pine tree. These short-legged balls of reddish fur were only a few weeks old. But they would grow quickly. Soon they would be bold enough to go outside the den. They would play and explore, smell new smells, and learn about being wolves. Their parents would teach them how to hunt.

In about a year, the cubs would leave their parents. In two years, they would have mates and families of their own. But their parents would stay together and have more cubs, for wolves usually stay with their mates for life.

The tiny cubs watched with bright eyes the things that were happening outside the den. In the twilight, their father and several other wolves were getting ready to hunt. The big wolves wagged their tails and playfully leaped at each other. After a while, they lifted their pointed noses to the sky and howled—long wails that floated off on the wind.

The howling went on for several minutes. Then the pups' father and his companions trotted off. The pups' mother, who had been howling with the others, returned to the den. At once, the pups began to climb and scramble playfully over her.

Meanwhile, the hunters trotted through the darkness, looking for food. They were also doing the job that nature had given them—the job of helping to keep things in balance. When the wolves found a herd of deer, they would chase them. If there was a weak or sick animal in the herd, the wolves would go after it because it couldn't run as fast as the others. By killing sick, unhealthy animals, wolves help the herds of deer stay strong and healthy. And the wolves also keep the herds from becoming so large that they eat up too many plants and spoil the land.

Actually, deer are not a red wolf's only food. Red wolves also eat rabbits, raccoons, and large furry rodents called nutria. In the places where they live, wolves are a great help in keeping such animals from increasing too much. That's a very good thing, because too many such animals can spoil large areas of land very quickly.

For hundreds of years, people all over the world have believed that wolves are cruel, bloodthirsty beasts. There are many fairy tales and old reports of wolves attacking people and eating them. Today, scientists know that most of these reports are not true. Many scientists and natural- ists have spent months living near wolves to study them. But they were never attacked or threatened. They found that wolves are smart, brave, good-natured animals that seem curious about people.

But people have feared and hated wolves for a long time. Wolves have been hunted, trapped, and poisoned. Governments have even paid money for every wolf that was killed.

At one time, red wolves lived throughout eastern North America. A much larger species—gray wolves (also called timber wolves and tundra wolves)—lived in almost every part of North America and on most continents of the world. Gray wolves became endangered for a time, but since the 1970's, many governments have begun to pro- tect them. Now their numbers have increased and they are no longer endangered.

The red wolf's condition, however, is still very serious. In fact, red wolves became extinct in the wild in 1980.

But conservationists raised some red wolves in captivity and released them into the wild in 1987. This group, which has now grown to more than 100, lives in northeastern North Carolina.

Today, the red wolf's biggest danger is not hunters. Instead, scientists are concerned that if red wolves mate with coyotes—which also live in North Carolina—they will lose the characteristics that make them unique. Researchers estimate that today, at least 300 red wolves live in the wild in North Carolina and in captivity in other parts of the United States.

⚠ **The polar bear**

The world of the polar bear is the frozen Arctic region around the North Pole. Here, these big, white giants roam alone over vast fields of snow-covered ice. Very good swimmers, they often ride ice floes across wide stretches of open ocean.

Most polar bears stay on the move all year long. But females with babies stay in dens during the winter. Before the dark, winter days begin, the female digs a deep hole in the snow. Down in this snowy cave, her cubs are born. Mother and babies spend the winter months cuddled together. The mother dozes most of the time. She does not eat at all, but lives on the stored-up fat in her body. The cubs live on her milk.

While mothers and cubs stay in their winter dens, other polar bears roam through the cold darkness. They search for holes in the ice that show where seals are. The seals swimming below the ice make these holes so they can come up to fill their lungs with air. A polar bear will wait for hours at one of these breathing holes. When a seal pops its head up, the bear scoops the seal out of the water with one swipe of its mighty paw.

Although polar bears will eat roots, berries, and plants in spring and summer, they are mostly meat-eaters. In fact, they are one of the biggest of all meat-eating animals. A full-grown male polar bear is usually about 7 or 8 feet (2 or 2.5 meters) long and 5 feet (1.5 meters) high. Some are even more than 12 feet (3.6 meters) long.

Polar bears have lived in the frozen north for thousands of years. But now, several dangers are threatening the bears. People hunt them for food, for their fur, and for other body parts. The seals and other animals that polar bears eat have absorbed poisonous pollutants. When the bears eat them, they become poisoned, too. And, as the climate becomes warmer and the ice melts for longer periods of time, polar bears are no longer able to use the ice floes as they hunt. Their way of life is threatened, and scientists are concerned that they will not be able to survive.

# ⚠ The Florida bonneted bat

any people are afraid of bats. Bats come out mostly at night. They may have strangely wrinkled faces. And some of them (vampire bats) feed on blood from birds and other animals. But bats also do many things that help people, such as controlling insects and *pollinating flowers* (helping them to reproduce).

Today, many kinds of bats are threatened. They are dying in large numbers from a disease called white-nose syndrome. They are also losing their habitat and being poisoned by pesticides.

One kind of bat, the Florida bonneted bat, is now critically endangered. Bonneted bats have large ears that hug their heads the way a bonnet hugs a woman's or a baby's face.

The Florida bonneted bat is one of the largest bats in North America. When its wings are spread out, they can stretch to 20 inches (51 centimeters). But this bat's furry, brownish-gray body is tiny—only about 3 to 4 inches (8 to 10 centimeters) long. It weighs only about 1.5 ounces (43 grams).

The Florida bonneted bat likes to *roost* (settle for sleep) in *Spanish tile* (reddish clay) roofs, in hollows found in old trees, and occasionally in the leaves of palm trees. It comes out at night to eat insects, which it finds through echolocation. Echolocation involves the use of echoes of sounds a bat makes to figure out where something is.

The Florida bonneted bat was once common along the eastern coast of Florida. Since the 1960's, it has only been seen in the Miami metropolitan area and near Fort Myers, on Florida's western coast.

Researchers think that there may be only about 100 Florida bonneted bats left. The old trees that these bats like to roost in are being cut down to make way for building projects. The insects—such as mosquitoes—that are the bats' main food increasingly contain pesticide. Eating the poisoned mosquitoes makes it harder for the bats to reproduce.

Conservationists would like to help Florida bonneted bats survive. However, as of the early 2000's, they were having a hard time finding enough of the bats to learn how to help them.

# ⚠ The black-footed ferret

**B**lack-footed ferrets were once widespread in the grasslands of central North America. The grasslands stretch across the Great Plains, from northern Canada to New Mexico and Texas. The ferrets *preyed on* (hunted and ate) the chubby, black-tailed prairie dogs that lived in the grasslands in underground burrows. Black-footed ferrets not only ate black-tailed prairie dogs, they lived in their burrows, too.

However, beginning in the late 1800's, ranchers started to kill black-tailed prairie dogs, which they considered pests. With its food supply drastically cut, the black-footed ferret almost disappeared as well. In fact, by 1987, scientists had classified black-footed ferrets as extinct in the wild. A small group of black-footed ferrets had been captured in Wyoming and kept in captivity but, by 1985, only 18 of them remained.

Conservationists worked closely with zookeepers to help black-footed ferrets reproduce. Then, from 1991 to 2008, they began to reintroduce black-footed ferrets into the places they once lived. Now, a few groups of the animals—about 500 or so adult ferrets—live in eight central and western states.

Black-footed ferrets are closely related to domestic ferrets, which people often keep as pets. Both kinds of ferrets have long, slim bodies and short legs. Domestic ferrets have fur that can range from nearly white to nearly black in color. Most of them are cream-colored, with dark feet, a dark tail, and a "mask" of dark fur around the eyes. They grow to be about 25 inches (64 centimeters) long.

Black-footed ferrets are a little shorter than domestic ferrets. Their fur is usually a dull yellow, with black feet, a black tail tip, and black fur around the eyes.

Black-tailed prairie dogs are no longer considered endangered. But black-footed ferrets still are. Much of the vast grassland in which the ferrets once lived is now being used to grow crops. Whatever land remains is often separated into small pieces by developments. But scientists have not given up on the black-footed ferret. They are doing their best to help the species come back from the brink of extinction.

# ⚠ The island fox

The island fox is the smallest fox in North America. It is only about 12 inches (30 centimeters) tall and weighs about 5 pounds (2.3 kilograms). Its fur is gray on the back, reddish-brown on the sides, and white on the underside. Its face is patterned in gray, white, and reddish-brown.

The island fox likes to live in rocky areas that have a lot of dense, woody brush in which it can hide. It eats fruits and berries, birds' eggs, insects, and such small prey as deer mice.

Male and female island foxes become pairs for life. Around April each year, the mother fox makes a *den* (place in which she will give birth) in a hollow log or stump, or in a burrow that has been dug by another animal. She usually has two or three "pups" (as her babies are called) in the spring. One month later, the dark, furry pups come out of the den and start to explore the world. But they stay near their parents for several more months before going out to live on their own. By that time, their fur has begun to change to colors more like those of their parents.

Island foxes once lived on all eight of the Channel Islands. These islands lie off the southern coast of California, between Santa Barbara and San Diego. Scientists believe that American Indians introduced the foxes to the islands.

Today, the island fox lives on only six of the largest islands—Santa Cruz, Santa Rosa, San Clemente, San Nicolas, and San Miguel. There are so few island foxes left that the species is considered critically endangered. One of the reasons its numbers have shrunk so much is that the small fox serves as prey for the large golden eagle. Another reason is that many foxes have died from a disease called canine distemper. On the island of Santa Catalina, nearly all of the island fox population died of the disease.

Conservationists are trying to help the island fox in several ways. They capture golden eagles and move them to northern California to live. They have also brought bald eagles to live on the islands instead. Although golden eagles and bald eagles are both large birds, golden eagles are more likely to feed on island foxes while bald eagles most often eat fish.

In addition, on the islands that have the fewest foxes, conservationists have set up special centers. There, the foxes are closely watched to be sure they do not become sick from canine distemper and to be sure that golden eagles do not catch them. When the groups of foxes at these centers become large enough, they are released into the wild. So one day, island foxes may again be plentiful on the Channel Islands.

# ⚠ The whooping crane

*er-loo! Ker-lee-oo!* The loud cry of the whooping cranes rings through the air like a bugle call. It is spring, and the big birds are rising up into the sky to begin their long journey to the north.

In winter, the whooping cranes live in a tiny, marshy place on the coast of Texas. In spring, the whole whooping crane flock flies to a wild part of northern Canada. They spend the summer in a wet, marshy place like the one in Texas. There the cranes mate, build their nests, lay their eggs, and hatch their baby chicks. In autumn, the cranes fly south, back to Texas.

The whooping crane is a big, grand bird. It is the tallest bird in North America—often up to 5 feet (1.5 meters) tall. When a big whooping crane spreads its wings, they may measure more than 7 feet (2 meters) from tip to tip. With its long legs, a whooping crane easily wades in shallow water to look for food. It eats frogs, crayfish, shellfish, snakes, many kinds of insects, and several kinds of plants.

In the mid-1800's, there were many whooping cranes in the wild parts of North America. But more and more people moved into the places where the cranes lived. The big birds were hunted and shot by the hundreds. Their eggs were stolen from their nests. Finally, there were fewer than 100 whoopers left.

Today, there are about 300 of these beautiful big birds in the wild. The United States and Canadian governments protect them. Whooping cranes are still in danger—but there is hope for them. In fact, scientists helped to establish a small second group of whoopers, which migrate from Wisconsin to Florida and back again every year.

## ⚠ The giant kangaroo rat

t's neither giant nor a kangaroo. It leaves its den for less than two hours a day, but it works like a farmer building haystacks out of dried grasses from which it harvests seeds. And it communicates with others of its kind by thumping its feet. The giant kangaroo rat is an amazing creature!

The giant kangaroo rat is one *species* (kind) of kangaroo rat. It is large for a kangaroo rat, which is why it is called "giant." And it is called a "kangaroo" rat because of its long, powerful hind legs, which it uses for jumping, and the pouch in its cheeks in which it carries seeds. Its body is covered with yellowish or brownish fur on top and white fur underneath.

Kangaroo rats live in the deserts of the southwestern United States and Mexico. The giant kangaroo rat, however, lives in only one small area of California, north of Los Angeles. There, it has become endangered because about 98 percent of its habitat is now used for farming.

The giant kangaroo rat can grow up to 14 inches (36 centimeters) long, including its tail. Its tail helps it to balance as it jumps. At top speeds, giant kangaroo rats can travel at almost 10 feet (3 meters) per second.

Giant kangaroo rats are mostly solitary creatures. They come out of their dens only at night, when it is cooler. Then, they gather seeds, stuff them into their cheek pouches, and bring them back to the den. They dry the seeds by either building haystacks out of seed-containing grasses or burying other kinds of seeds in the ground. When the seeds are dry enough, the giant kangaroo rat brings them into the den for storage. Seeds are not only the animal's food, but also its drink—it gets all the water it needs from the seeds.

Although the giant kangaroo rat does not like to live with others of its kind, it does have a way of communicating with them. It uses a variety of foot thumpings to identify neighbors, protect its territory, and look for a mate. Giant kangaroo rats even try to scare away snakes with foot thumping!

Some of the giant kangaroo rats' territory is in a protected area where farming is not allowed. But if we want to save the giant kangaroo rat, we'll need to do much more to protect the land it needs for making its dens and finding food.

# ⚠ The California condor

he body of a dead sheep lay in a grassy meadow on a mountainside. Two jet-black ravens
perched on the body, tearing bits of flesh from it.

Suddenly, a great shadow glided over the body.
Overhead, a big bird soared on wings that stretched
more than 9 feet (3 meters) from tip to tip. Slowly,
the bird circled down and landed a short distance
from the dead sheep. With its wings held partly out
for balance, it waddled to the body.

At once, the ravens flew away. The big bird bent
over the sheep. With its sharp, curved beak, it hungri-
ly ripped off chunks of meat. This bird, a California
condor, is one of the largest flying birds in the world.
It feeds chiefly on the flesh of dead animals.

California condors spend much of their time sitting
in the sun on branches of dead trees or on rocky cliff
tops. They often bathe in nearby streams. When they
get hungry, they fly over the countryside looking for
the bodies of dead cattle, sheep, deer, or other big
animals. When a condor drops down out of the sky to
eat, most other birds that may be eating already will
quickly get out of its way. But condors share their
finds with each other.

The California condor once lived in most of western North America. By 1987, the last six birds left in
the wild were taken to a sanctuary in Los Padres
National Forest in southern California. They are protected by law. But even so, they were sometimes
shot. Scientists helped the group to grow until, in the
2000's, there were more than 300 birds. Some of
these have now been returned to the wild.

# ⚠ The ivory-billed woodpecker

*rnithologists* (bird experts) throughout the world were thrilled in 2005. A team of scientists reported that in 2004 they had seen an ivory-billed woodpecker in an area known as the Big Woods in eastern Arkansas. They had even videotaped it! But how could that be? Everyone believed the ivory-billed woodpecker had been extinct for at least 50 years.

Amateur bird watchers and expert scientists alike flocked to the spot. Conservationists spent more than $10 million over five years searching for the bird. But in the end, no one could find any proof that the bird still existed. Even the videotape was not clear. Some experts thought the bird the scientists filmed could have been a very similar, common woodpecker called the pileated woodpecker.

Why all the fuss about a bird? Those who had seen an ivory-billed woodpecker reported that it was a magnificent creature. Its nickname was the Lord God Bird because people who saw it often cried out "Lord God, what a bird!"

With an average length of about 20 inches (50 centimeters), the ivory-billed woodpecker was the third-largest woodpecker in the world. It had a heavy white bill that was not really ivory (of which elephant and walrus tusks are made), yellow eyes, and white wing feathers on a black body. The males had a pointy red crest on their heads. In flight, the birds moved as swiftly as arrows and made a great deal of noise. They used their hard bills to pry bark from trees to uncover the beetle *larvae* (early stage of insect life) they loved to eat.

At one time, ivory-billed woodpeckers were common in the southeastern United States, from North Carolina to Florida and from the east coast to Texas and Oklahoma. But they began to disappear as the old, hardwood forests filled with beetle larvae were cut down. The last scientifically verified photographs of ivory-billed woodpeckers were taken in the United States in 1938 and in Cuba in 1948.

Today, some scientists think there is still hope that the ivory-billed woodpecker is not extinct. But many scientists believe that there probably are not enough such birds to bring the species back to a healthy number.

# ⚠ The river turtle

or weeks, a steady rain has poured down from a dark sky. It rattles on the leaves of plants and hisses into the broad, gray river. So much rain has fallen, the river is overflowing its banks. Much of the land on both sides of the river is already under water.

Thousands of huge turtles live in the watery, muddy land near the river. These big turtles have round shells up to 3 feet (0.9 meter) wide. Unlike sea turtles, which have flippers, river turtles have small feet that stick out from under their shell. But similarly to sea turtles, they have heads that they can *retract* (pull back in) when they are frightened. Some river turtles live for as long as 30 years. They move very slowly, constantly searching for fruits, flowers, and soft, leafy plants to eat.

At last, the rain begins to let up. The rainy season is ending. When the rain does stop, the hot, tropical sun comes out again. Slowly, the water in the river begins to go down.

Now the turtles stop eating and head for the river. Soon, the water is filled with turtles, all swimming in the same direction. Often they must battle against strong currents and make their way through rushing rapids. But nothing stops them. They swim on until they reach their goal—some little islands in the river. Each year, this is where they mate and lay their eggs.

For several days, the female turtles lie on the beach at the water's edge, basking in the hot sun. Then, one night, they all begin to crawl farther up on the beach to lay their eggs. The beach is covered with turtles, each one looking for just the right place.

When a turtle decides she has found the right place, she digs a hole in the sand. This hole is as wide as she is—about 3 feet (0.9 meter) in diameter. She may lay 80 or more round, soft-shelled eggs in the hole. All in all, tens of thousands of eggs are laid on the same beach on a single night. Then, the turtles cover the eggs, smoothing out the sand as they try to hide their nests. When this is done, the mother turtles crawl back down to the river and swim away.

Day after day, the hot sun bakes down on the sand. About forty-five days after the eggs are laid, the tiny baby turtles begin to hatch. They dig their way up out of the sand. Soon the beach is covered with tiny, scurrying shapes. Thousands of baby turtles are rushing down to the water. But many of them never make it. Swarms of vultures and other birds swoop down to gobble up the tiny turtles. Even when the babies reach the water, they aren't safe. Crocodiles and fish wait to eat as many as they can.

Various kinds of river turtles have lived in Central and South America for millions of years. Many baby turtles were eaten each year, but enough got away so that there were always a great many turtles.

At least there used to be. And there would be still if it weren't for people, because people love to eat turtle eggs. For several hundred years, people have come to the islands and taken millions of turtle eggs before they could hatch. (Although the mother turtles think their nests are hidden, the locations of turtle nesting sites are well known to local people.) Now, there are many places where there are no turtles. After millions of years, the turtles are in danger—because of people.

# ⚠ The brown spider monkey

I t swings through the trees with the greatest of ease—even though it's one of the largest primates in South America. It's the brown spider monkey! (Primates are a group of mammals—warm-blooded animals—that includes human beings, apes, and monkeys.)

Spider monkeys include several different kinds of monkeys that live in tropical forests from Mexico to Bolivia. The brown spider monkey, is, of course, brown. It lives in Colombia and Venezuela.

Spider monkeys have four long, slender *limbs* (arms and legs), and a long tail that they use like a fifth limb. They can pick up objects with their tail. They can also use it to hang onto branches, which is why they can move through the treetops so quickly. In fact, spider monkeys don't usually walk or run. They travel by swinging from branch to branch.

Adult spider monkeys grow to about 2 feet (61 centimeters) long (without the tail) and weigh from 10 to 19 pounds (5 to 8.6 kilograms). They stay mostly in the treetops, where they find the fruit, seeds, young leaves, and flowers that they like to eat. People rarely see them on the forest floor.

Spider monkeys live in groups of up to 35 individuals. But they usually eat, sleep, and travel in smaller groups. The groups travel within a certain home range in the forest. Each female usually has a special area within that home range where she likes to stay.

Spider monkeys become adults at about the age of 4 or 5. When a female becomes pregnant, she carries the baby for more than 7 months. Mothers give birth to only one baby at a time, and the baby stays with its mother for about two years.

Brown spider monkeys have become critically endangered for two reasons. Their forest habitat is being chopped down to clear the land for cattle ranching; and people hunt brown spider monkeys for sport and for food. Conservationists are trying to have more of the monkeys' habitat set aside as national parks and reserves so that rangers can keep the brown spider monkey safe.

# ⚠ The giant armadillo

**T**he giant armadillo waddled along the sandy riverbank. It was searching for a place to dig itself a shelter. From time to time it reared up slightly to walk on its two back legs, with its front legs hanging down and barely touching the ground.

When the armadillo found a good spot, it began to dig. It was a wonderfully fast and skillful digger. Sand flew, and the hole grew quickly. As it dug, the armadillo uncovered a plump, wiggly worm, or a juicy insect. Then it used its long, narrow tongue to grab a quick snack. It would also gladly have eaten any snakes or spiders it found.

From the tip of its nose to the end of its tail, the giant armadillo is about 5 feet (1.5 meters) long. It weighs more than 130 pounds (59 kilograms). The big, sharp claws on its front feet are perfect for digging.

With its strong claws and shell of bumpy, bony armor, the giant armadillo looks like a fierce creature that can take good care of itself. But this big animal is really quite timid. If an enemy appears, the armadillo tries to run away and hide in a burrow rather than fight. And if it can't get away, it curls up in a ball and depends upon its thick skin and bony armor to save it.

There are not very many of these curious-looking, armor-plated animals. The forests where they live in several South American countries are being cleared, and sometimes the animals are hunted. Scientists fear that the giant armadillo is slowly being wiped out.

# ⚠ The chinchilla

The chinchilla is a member of the rodent family, which also includes mice and squirrels. It is a rodent with beautiful, shiny, blue-gray fur! Chinchillas are about 11 to 18 inches (28 to 46 centimeters) long, including the bushy tail. Their thick fur is so fine and silky that a coat made of chinchilla fur has sold for as much as $100,000!

Chinchillas need their thick fur to keep warm. They live high up in the snow-capped Andes Mountains. Little family groups of from two to five animals share burrows among the rocks. They sleep during the day and come out at night. Then they hop and scurry in search of grass, seeds, roots, moss, and any other plant food they can find. When a chinchilla eats, it sits up on its hind legs and tail, like a squirrel, and holds its food in its front paws.

The Spaniards who came to South America in the 1500's named the chinchilla after the Chincha Indians. Because of their beautiful fur, chinchillas were nearly wiped out by hunters and trappers by the 1940's. For many years, scientists thought chinchillas were extinct. Then a few were found and captured. These captives were the ancestors of thousands of chinchillas that are now raised on special ranches.

Because there are so many ranch chinchillas, the chinchilla family will probably never die out. But the wild chinchillas are still in great trouble. Although some countries have passed laws to protect them, there may not be enough wild chinchillas left to sur-vive—or enough habitat for them to survive in.

# ⚠ The spectacled bear

It's easy to see how the spectacled bear got its name. The circles of yellowish fur around its *eyes* make it look as if it is wearing a pair of enormous *spectacles* (an old-fashioned word for eyeglasses).

The spectacled bear is the only kind of wild bear that lives in South America. It is a small bear, about 5 feet (1.5 meters) long and weighing 200 to 300 pounds (91 to 140 kilograms). It lives in forests on the slopes of mountains. Not very much is known about the spectacled bear. It seems to be more of a plant-eater than other bears, feeding mostly on leaves, fruits, and roots.

Like most bears, the spectacled bear is a skillful climber. It sometimes stands upright, to pull leafy branches down to its mouth, but it often climbs trees for its food. It is fond of the leaves of a certain kind of palm tree. It climbs the tree, tears off branches, and lets them fall to the ground. Then it climbs down and eats the leaves off the branches. Some people think that spectacled bears build nests of twigs and branches, high in trees.

The spectacled bear is slowly disappearing. People hunt it and set traps for it. Its habitat is being destroyed as more roads are built through it and as forests are cut down to make way for farmland. There may be only a few thousand of these animals left.

# ⚠ The Baird's tapir

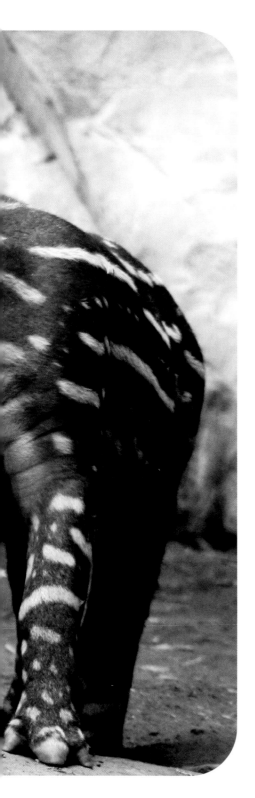

A tapir *(TAY puhr)* is a short, heavy animal that looks somewhat like a pig. But it is actually more closely related to the horse and rhinoceros.

There are several kinds of tapirs. One kind lives in Indonesia and Malaysia. The other kinds live in Central and South America. Baird's tapir lives in Central America and in the northern part of South America. It is the largest and heaviest of the American tapirs.

Baird's tapirs like to live near fresh water, in marshy and swampy places and in rain forests. They eat twigs, fruits, and leaves from the forest floor and plants that grow in water.

Adult tapirs grow to be about 6.5 feet (2 meters) long and can weigh as much as 660 pounds (300 kilograms). They have bristly, dark brown hair, a short tail, and a head that ends in a short trunk similar to an elephant's. Baby Baird's tapirs look very different than adult tapirs. They are born with reddish-brown hair that is covered with whitish streaks and spots. The streaks and spots disappear as the babies grow.

Today, there are fewer than 5,000 Baird's tapirs left in the wild. Their habitat is gradually being destroyed, and people hunt them for sport and for meat. In addition, Baird's tapirs reproduce very slowly. Mothers carry a baby for 13 months, have only one baby at a time, and then take care of the baby for two years before it is old enough to be on its own.

# ⚠ The golden poison frog

**F**or such a tiny creature, it sure packs a big wallop! The golden poison frog is less than 2 inches (5 centimeters) long. But its skin contains a *toxin* (poisonous substance) that can kill just about any animal foolish enough to eat it. (Only one type of snake has been known to eat the little frog and live.) Usually, the frog's bright golden color is enough to warn animals away.

The only places where golden poison frogs live are the warm, humid forests along the coast of the Pacific Ocean in Colombia. Indians who live in these rain forests smear the poison on darts and use it for hunting. When a poisoned dart strikes an animal, the animal's muscles and breathing become paralyzed, and the animal dies. Even human beings can die if just a tiny quantity of the poison—about the amount of two or three grains of table salt—touches an open cut on the skin or is swallowed. Scientists learned in the 2000's that the golden poison frog gets its poison from eating mites, tiny animals that live in the soil of the forest floor.

Golden poison frogs are endangered because their habitat is slowly being destroyed. They live in only five small areas in Colombia. The forests there are being cut down to make way for farmland and housing developments. Scientists hope that these areas can be set aside as nature reserves, so that the golden poison frog does not become extinct.

## ⚠ The golden lion tamarin

Golden lion tamarins are small South American monkeys that live in Brazil. Their yellow-gold fur is long and silky. Lion-like manes surround their little faces. Only about 12 inches (30 centimeters) long, golden lion tamarins have fluffy tails that are longer than they are.

These tiny creatures live in thick forests. Quick-moving and active, they dart and scurry and leap from branch to branch like golden blurs. They are also noisy, squeaking and chattering most of the time. They travel together in groups, searching for fruits, insects, tiny lizards, and small birds. When tamarins want to sleep or rest, they usually hide in the hollow of a tree.

Male golden lion tamarins make fine fathers. They carry the babies on their backs and help to feed them when they are old enough for solid food. A tamarin father squeezes bits of food between his fingers to make it soft before he gives it to his youngster. Even when a young tamarin is able to take care of itself, its father often seems to want to look after it!

Golden lion tamarins are endangered mainly because the forest where they live has been cut down to make room for sugar and coffee plantations and cattle ranches. Only about 20 percent of their habitat remains. Scientists estimate that about 1,000 golden lion tamarins remain in the wild.

⚠ **The sea otter**

own among the rocks and seaweed on the ocean floor, a sea otter searched for something to eat. Oh! The otter's sharp eyes saw a cluster of oysters huddled together on a boulder. In an instant, she scooped up two of them and tucked them under one of her front legs. Then she picked up a flat rock that lay in the sand. She tucked it under her other front leg.

With a whip of her flipper-shaped back feet, the otter shot up to the surface of the water. Popping out into the air, she rolled over onto her back and began to float. She put the flat rock on her chest. Then, taking one of the oysters between her paws, she smashed it down against the rock. After several whacks, the oyster cracked open. The otter happily gobbled up the soft, whitish meat inside the shell.

When she finished eating, she rolled over in the water to wash away scraps of food stuck to her fur. It is very important for a sea otter to keep its fur clean. The thick, brown fur traps a blanket of air all around the otter's body. This air helps the otter to float. It also protects the otter against cold. If the fur gets dirty or is stuck together, the otter cannot float. It may also die from the cold. So otters spend lots of time cleaning their fur.

Otters also spend lots of time eating. A full-grown otter, which may be 4 feet (1.2 meters) long, can eat more than 15 pounds (7 kilograms) of food a day. That's a lot more than you eat!

A mother otter usually has only one baby each time she gives birth. The mother and baby stay together for

about a year. The baby spends most of its time lying on its mother's chest, while she floats on her back. When the mother gets hungry, she pushes the baby into the water. While she dives down for food, the baby floats like a cork. Sometimes the mother wraps seaweed around the baby to keep it from floating too far away. Sea otters often wrap themselves in seaweed when they sleep, so they won't float too far from the place where they get their food.

Sea otters live in shallow water off parts of Alaska, California, and Oregon. They also live along the coasts of Canada, Japan, and Russia.

There used to be thousands of sea otters. But they were hunted for their fur, until they were nearly all gone. They are now in trouble because of water pollution, which gets their fur dirty and oily, and because they accidentally get caught in fishing nets. The otters are also in trouble because killer whales have begun to kill them as their other choices of food have disappeared. Unless we can find ways to help them, sea otters could easily become extinct.

# ⚠ The Antipodean albatross

An albatross is a very large bird. It lives most of its life at sea and comes to land only during its time for having babies. The Antipodean albatross is a kind of albatross that lives over the South Pacific Ocean. It breeds in the area of New Zealand, on the Antipodes Islands, the Auckland Islands, and Campbell Island.

The Antipodean albatross is about 43 inches (110 centimeters) long. It has a mixture of chocolate brown and white feathers covering its body and a pink bill. When the bird is in flight, its wingspan can be nearly 10 feet (3 meters) wide.

For most of the year, Antipodean albatrosses stay at sea. They can glide for long periods of time on their huge wings, using very little energy. That is a useful trait, because they usually have to travel far in search of food. They look for dead squid floating on the surface of the sea. They also eat fish and *cuttlefish* (a soft, boneless animal similar to the squid).

When it is time to mate, both male and female albatrosses perform an elaborate courtship dance. Two birds that have chosen to pair up will stay together for life. They bow to each other, snap their bills and touch them together, shake their heads, and *preen* (smooth or arrange their feathers with their beaks). They build their nest out in the open, usually among grasses or shrubs. The female lays one egg, and both parents take turns sitting on it. When the baby albatross—called a chick—hatches, both parents find food and bring it back for the newborn.

Conservationists are concerned about the Antipodean albatross because the number of chicks born each year keeps getting smaller. Wild pigs on the islands on which the albatross breeds eat many eggs before they can hatch. *Feral* (wild) cats kill large numbers of chicks as well. Grown albatrosses are often killed by the long lines that fishing crews use to catch tuna.

# ⚠ The northern rockhopper penguin

Penguins are birds that cannot fly. They spend most of their time in the ocean and return to land only to raise their young. On land, their short legs and tall, torpedo-like bodies cause them to waddle when they walk. But they can walk about as fast as human beings can, and they are excellent swimmers.

The northern rockhopper penguin is one of the smaller kinds of penguins. It lives north of Antarctica, on islands in the South Atlantic Ocean and the southern Indian Ocean.

Northern rockhoppers are only about 22 inches (55 centimeters) tall and weigh only about 5 ½ pounds (2.5 kilograms). Their bellies are white and their backs and flippers are black. They have red eyes. Above each eye is a yellow stripe that ends in long, yellow feathers that form a crest. On the back of the head is a crest of black feathers.

Northern rockhoppers spend most of their time at sea, eating such crustaceans as crabs, crayfish, lobsters, and shrimp. But in July of each year, they head to the islands north of Antarctica to breed. The birds gather in large colonies that may contain thousands of nests. Breeding pairs not only return to the same area each year, they even return to the same nest. They repair the old nest with new pebbles, sticks, and grasses. Then, the female lays two eggs. (Usually, though, northern rockhoppers only raise one chick.)

For several weeks, both parents stay at the nest, keeping the eggs warm. Then, the female goes off for several days to eat. When she returns, the male goes off to find food. The male then finishes the job, staying at the nest until the chick hatches and while it is very young. The female brings food back to the nest for the chick. When the chick is a little older, it joins a *crèche* (a small group of young chicks). Both parents head out to sea to catch enough food for themselves and their growing youngster.

Scientists are not sure why northern rockhopper penguins have become endangered. But they do know that their numbers have fallen severely since the 1950's. Northern rockhoppers get caught in large commercial fishing nets. Their eggs are eaten by predators that people have introduced to their breeding islands. And their food supply has dwindled because of large commercial fishing operations and the gradual warming of waters around Antarctica.

Conservationists have worked to make some of the northern rockhoppers' breeding islands nature reserves. They hope that such a move will help protect these small, colorful creatures.

⚠ **The blue whale**

The surface of the ocean is calm and quiet. Suddenly, an enormous, bluish-gray body pushes up out of the water! A thick spout of steam hisses high into the air. A blue whale has come up to "blow."

Whales look like giant fish, but they are really mammals—like dogs, cows, horses, and human beings. They cannot breathe under water. A blue whale can hold its breath under water for about 20 minutes. The air in its lungs gets hot and steamy. When the whale surfaces, it blows the air out through two holes in the top of its head. This hot air makes a great fountain of steam when it shoots out into the cold ocean air.

The blue whale is the biggest of all animals. A full-grown blue whale may be nearly 100 feet (30.5 meters) long and weigh 150 tons (135 metric tons)—that's heavier than the heaviest dinosaur that ever lived! When a blue whale is born, it is already bigger than a full-grown elephant!

In summer, blue whales stay in cold water near the North or South poles. In winter, they move into warmer parts of the ocean. They travel alone or in pairs, following the huge clouds of tiny shrimp-like creatures called krill that drift in the ocean. A blue whale eats thousands of pounds of these creatures each day. To eat, a whale just swims into a crowd of krill with its mouth open. As the whale closes its mouth, its tongue pushes the water out. This leaves only the krill, which the whale then swallows.

Blue whales have been hunted until only a small number of them are left. Even though commercial whaling has been banned since 1986, a few countries still hunt whales for other reasons. Many scientists fear there is no way to keep these magnificent creatures from becoming extinct.

# Why Is It Happening?

*"We are the volcano, we are the asteroid. We are the ones who are driving a lot of these species to extinction."*

**Jeff Corwin**
Corwin is a wildlife biologist and the Emmy-award winning host of the cable televison wildlife documentary *The Jeff Corwin Experience.*

# The Most Dangerous Enemy

The great African rhinoceros dozed in a pile of powdery dust beside an old, crumbling termite hill. It lay on its stomach, with its front legs tucked under its chest, its chin on the ground. The thick, gray skin of the black rhinoceros was as wrinkled and creased as the bark on a gnarled old tree trunk.

This was the dry season. No rain had fallen for weeks. When there were no muddy puddles to wallow in, this big dust pile was the rhino's favorite place. The big animal came here each day to doze from midmorning until late afternoon. Near sunset, it would trot off into the thickets, to graze on leaves most of the night.

Three small, brownish birds moved about on the rhino's broad back. Occasionally, the birds dug their beaks into the rhino's skin. These were oxpeckers, little birds that often stay with rhinoceroses. They feed on the insects that live on a rhino's body.

The oxpeckers had been feeling nervous for some time. Something was wrong, but they had not yet discovered what it was. From time to time they would cock their heads and peer with bright eyes across the great yellow plain that stretched out around the termite hill. Was there a strange scent in the air? Was something out on the plain moving toward them?

There was! Suddenly they saw it. They began to screech and chatter with nervous excitement. All together, they fluttered up into the air.

The sudden commotion woke the rhino instantly. The big beast's eyes opened and it scrambled to its feet. It was not frightened. There were no animals on the great plain that could do harm to the huge, horned creature. Even a family of lions would slink out of its way if it moved toward them. But all the rhino's wild animal senses warned it of danger.

Something was approaching. The rhino's nearsighted eyes could see nothing but a blur moving slowly toward it. But to its keen nose there came a sharp, unfamiliar smell. The rhino hesitated, as if deciding whether to lower its head and charge, or simply turn and run away.

*Crack!*

A single rifle shot echoed over the plain. The rhino fell to its knees. For nearly a minute it remained unmoving, frozen in surprise and pain. Then, with a great thump, it flopped over on its side and lay still.

The man with the rifle hurried to the rhino's body. Quickly, he cut the two horns from the dead animal's nose and stuffed them into a bag slung over his shoulder. Then, bending low, he scurried toward a line of scrub trees in the distance.

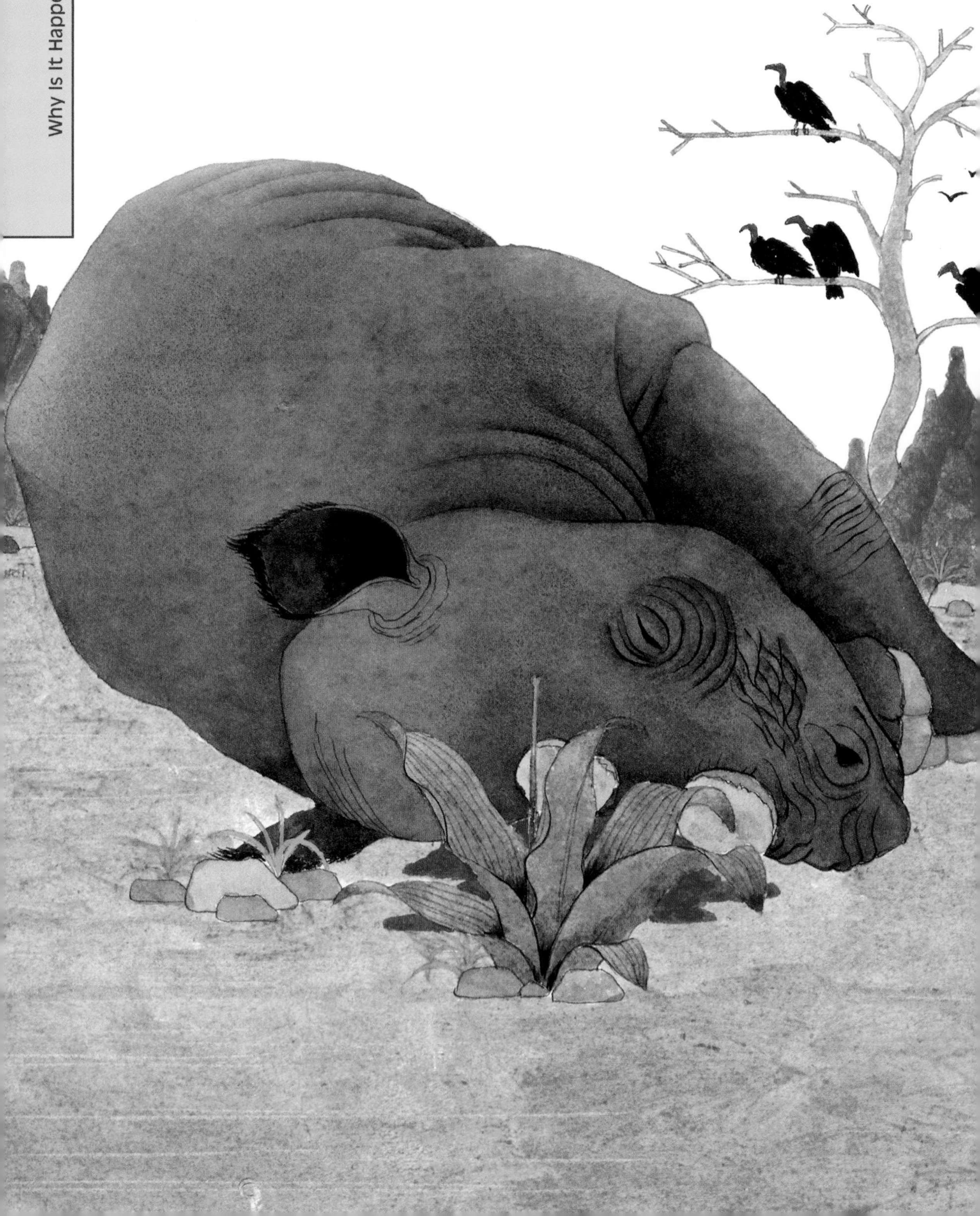

Panting, he knelt behind some bushes and looked back anxiously across the plain. He was looking for a telltale cloud of dust that would mean a car or truck was speeding toward him. What he had just done was against the law. If he were caught he would be put in prison for a long time. But every rhinoceros horn he could get was worth its weight in gold! People in many parts of Asia would pay well for just a tiny piece of rhino horn. These people believe it is a magical sort of medicine.

Satisfied that no one was coming, the man rose to his feet and set out toward his camp, which was hidden a few miles away. He had more horns there, from other rhinos he had killed. It's worth the risk, thought the man—if I can get enough horns I'll be rich! He grinned at the thought.

The rhino's big, gray body lay motionless in the dust. It was covered with a cloud of noisy, buzzing flies. Soon, vultures would come drifting down on stiff wings to squawk and squabble over the body.

The rhino had not been killed to feed hungry people. It had not been killed because it was dangerous or troublesome. It had not even been killed for sport. It had been killed because its horns are worth money. It did not matter to the man who had killed it that there are not many of these big, wonderful creatures left. He would have killed it even if he had known that it was the very last rhinoceros in the world.

Wild animals face many dangers. Other animals may hunt them for food. They may die from lack of food or water. They may be killed by forest fires, drowned in floods, or trapped in quicksand. But none of these things can destroy an entire species of animal. Only people can do this. People kill animals for their skins or horns. People take over animals' lands for farms, mines, and factories. People pollute the air, earth, and water with chemicals, oil, and garbage. A wild animal's most dangerous enemy is people.

A hyena attacks a wildebeest on the plains of Kenya. Animals that prey on others help to preserve the balance of nature.

# Too Much Killing

Beneath a pale moon, shadowy shapes glided across the African plain. A frightening, chattering laugh broke the night's stillness. The hyenas were hunting!

As the hyenas moved toward a small herd of wildebeests, they scared the big, shaggy animals. The wildebeests ran for their lives. The hyenas raced after them. Quickly, they closed in on a young wildebeest that was not as fast as the others. The hyenas pulled it down, killed it, and began to feast on its flesh.

Hyenas and hawks, foxes and frogs, spiders and snakes, lions and lizards, dolphins and dragonflies—all these, and many other animals, are hunters. They hunt and kill other creatures for food. Some people think of animals that kill others as "bad," but that isn't true. Animals that kill others only do what they must do to stay alive.

As a matter of fact, the world *needs* hunting animals. They do a very important job. If meat-eaters, such as hyenas, did not kill some of the plant-eating animals, such as wildebeests, there would soon be too many plant-eaters. The plant-eaters would eat up all the plants in places where they live. Before long, the land would turn into a desert. Then the plant-eaters would starve. But all over the world, meat-eating animals keep other animals from increasing too much. And as long as the plant-eaters don't increase too much, the meat-eaters can't increase, either. So this kind of hunting helps keep nature in balance.

A fin whale—a species that is endangered—lies on the deck of a whaling ship near Iceland.

People also hunt. They hunt for sport and for food. The kind of hunting that many people do does not upset the balance of nature, either. In many countries, people are allowed to hunt only animals that are plentiful. And they can shoot only a small number of these animals. There is no danger that all the animals will be killed off by this kind of hunting. Also, people pay money for permission to hunt. This money helps take care of places where wild animals can live.

But some kinds of hunting *do* upset the balance of nature. In many parts of the world, animals are being wiped out by hunting. In some countries, governments are taking action to protect animals. Some laws allow hunters to kill only limited numbers of certain animals, if they are in danger of dying out. In Canada, for example, only people who have a government permit may hunt polar bears. In Australia, the government limits the number of kangaroo killings. And the International Whaling Commission allows only three countries—Iceland, Japan, and Norway—to hunt for whales.

In many parts of the world, killing endangered animals is entirely forbidden by the law. Hunters who kill these animals are punished if they are caught. They may have to pay a fine or even go to jail. National parks and wildlife reserves have game wardens or rangers who arrest hunters who break the law.

Even when it is against the law to hunt certain kinds of animals, there are hunters who pay no attention to the law. They hunt tigers, leopards, otters, and other animals for their valuable fur. The hunters sell the skins of these animals to companies that make clothes, rugs, and gifts from them. Crocodiles are hunted for their skins, too. The skins are used to make shoes, belts, and purses. Hunters kill rhinoceroses for their horns and elephants for their tusks. The horns are used in traditional Oriental medicines

Ivory tusks that Kenyan government officials have seized from poachers lie heaped in a stack. They will be burned so that no one can sell them.

and valuable ivory objects are made from the tusks.

In some countries, laws have been passed to stop people from selling the meat, skin, or any other part of an endangered animal. This means that hunters who have been making money by killing lots of animals will no longer be able to sell the body parts of the animals they kill. If they cannot make

money by killing animals, they may stop hunting them.

Laws such as these may stop much of the killing of endangered animals. Then, perhaps, the animals will be able to grow in numbers. They will no longer be in danger of becoming extinct.

There is another kind of hunting that had nearly wiped out many kinds of animals. These animals are not hunted for their skins, or meat, or horns, or tusks. They are not even hunted as a sport. They are killed off simply because some people think they are harmful or cause problems. Numbers of prairie dogs, wolves, mountain lions, and many other kinds of animals in North America and other parts of the world have been killed because they are thought to be "pests."

But we are now finding out that many of these "pests" are not pests at all. Some of them are really very helpful. We have learned that prairie dogs help to make the land better for growing things. And we have found that wolves and mountain lions do an important job by controlling the numbers of plant-eating animals. Many animal "pests" are no longer hunted and poisoned. Instead, we are trying to save them.

Police officers in China question a shopkeeper selling goods made from the fur of endangered snow leopards.

A mother orangutan and her baby swing through the treetops of their forest home.

# Changes in the Land

The great, green forest stretched for miles and miles. Millions of huge trees, wrapped in thick vines, crowded together. The leaves formed a roof that shut out the sunlight and held in the heat. This made the forest hot and damp and dark.

In the upper treetops, where the sun was bright, lived the large, red-furred apes called orangutans. The treetops were their houses, streets, and grocery stores. The orangs slept in the trees, moved through them as easily as you walk on a sidewalk, and got all their food from them.

The orangs were always on the move. As soon as they ate the best leaves, juiciest buds, and ripest fruits in one place, the apes moved to another place. There was always plenty of food to be found in the enormous forest. Even in the places where all the food had been eaten, it would soon grow back again.

As families of orangutans moved about through the huge forest, they often met each other. This was how the young orangs found mates and started new families.

For thousands of years the orangutans lived this way in their forest home. There was plenty of food. They had no enemies. There was a lot of room in the great forest. So there were many thousands of orangs.

Then, people came. They cut down the great trees. The wood was needed to build houses. The land where the trees stood was needed for farms.

Soon the forest was much smaller. And so was the number of orangutans. There was not enough room for all of them any more. There was not enough food to go around.

Some of the orangs were forced out of the forest, into places where they could not live. Others were left in tiny groups in small bits of forest that had not been cleared.

In many parts of the Amazon rain forest, people have cleared all of the trees, leaving no places for animals to live and to find food.

But these small patches of forest were widely separated. The orangs living in these small areas were cut off from others of their kind. Now, many of them would never find mates and raise families.

Most wild animals can live only in places where the plants or animals they need also live. Many animals need lots of room to search for food and find mates. If people take over and change most of the land, many kinds of animals will die out.

Another kind of danger often comes to animals when people move into their lands. The people sometimes bring other animals with them—animals from other parts of the world. This often causes serious trouble.

Little birds called Stephens Island wrens once lived on a tiny, rocky island in the Pacific Ocean. These plump birds had brownish feathers, short tails, and wings that were too small for flying. There weren't many wrens, because there wasn't much food for them on the island. But the wrens lived very well. There were no animals that hunted them, and no animals could get to the island.

But if animals couldn't get to the island, people in boats could. One day, people came. They built a lighthouse on the island in 1894. Then the man in charge of the lighthouse came—and he brought a cat with him.

The cat soon discovered the wrens. It began to hunt them. The wrens were helpless. They had never been hunted by an enemy before. They couldn't fly and they didn't know how to hide. Before long, the cat had killed them all. The Stephens Island wren is extinct.

Every place in the world has its own kinds of animals. If other kinds of animals are brought from somewhere else, they often cause trouble. Sometimes the new animals hunt and kill many of the native animals, as the cat did. Sometimes they take over the native animals' food.

The tuatara, a small reptile, was saved when people set aside islands on which no other animals were permitted.

There is really only one good way to protect animals from such "outsiders." The "outsiders" must be kept away. Little reptiles called tuataras were nearly wiped out because settlers brought rats and other new animals to the islands where the tuataras lived. The "outsiders" ate the tuataras and wiped them out on many of the islands.

But then, a few islands where tuataras still lived were turned into protected places. No "outsider" animals were permitted on the islands. This saved the tuataras.

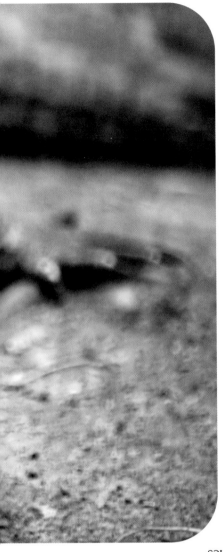

Turning places where wild animals live into protected places is the best way to save animals from all kinds of problems. Many countries have made parts of forests, plains, and mountains into protected places called national parks or animal reserves.

In most parks and reserves, no trees can be cut down, no houses or factories can be built, no hunting is allowed, and no animals can be brought in from somewhere else. The land is kept wild, and the animals in these places are protected. On the next few pages, you can see what some of these parks and reserves look like and the kinds of animals that live in them.

It is not always possible to save places for animals in their own lands. So some animals that are in danger are moved to new homes. But the new homes may be thousands of miles away in other countries. The San Diego Wild Animal Park is such a place. This animal reserve is in southern California. It is much like the land in parts of Asia and Africa. Many kinds of African and Asian animals have been brought to the park to live.

The park is a kind of zoo. But it is more than just a place where people can look at animals. It's a way of saving animals. Scientists at the park study the animals to learn more about how they live. Some of the animals in the San Diego Wild Animal Park are in danger in their own countries. But in the park they are protected. They are not kept in cages, but are out in the open where they have room to move around. They are able to have babies and increase their numbers. This doesn't always happen when animals are kept in cages in ordinary zoos.

There are other places like the San Diego Wild Animal Park. Even though certain kinds of wild animals may become extinct in their own lands, some will be safe and sound in new homes in other lands.

## Great Barrier Reef Marine Park, Australia

This park, which protects the world's largest system of coral reefs, is home to fish, turtles, sharks, and sea mammals called dugongs, as well as the thousands of tiny ocean animals called corals.

## Banff National Park, Canada

Banff, the oldest national park in Canada, lies on the eastern side of the Rocky Mountains in the province of Alberta. Elk *(inset)*, bighorn sheep, and black and grizzly bears are among the animals that live in the park.

**Maasai Mara Game Reserve, Kenya**

An African elephant plucks leaves from a shrub on the reserve, home to a spectacular variety of wild animals, including rhinos, cheetahs, giraffes, hippopotamuses, and zebras.

## Corcovado National Park, Costa Rica

A Baird's tapir—an endangered species —searches for food in the shade of a tree in Corcovado National Park. Costa Rica's many national parks attract thousands of tourists each year.

## Yellowstone National Park, United States

An American buffalo, or bison, grazes in Yellowstone, the oldest national park in the world. Bison were hunted almost to extinction in the 1800's. Now the animals are protected in many national and state parks and reserves.

## Woolong National Nature Reserve, China

A giant panda lounges in a meadow on a nature reserve. Much of the panda's natural habitat has been destroyed, but the Chinese government has set aside reserves to try to protect the animals in the wild.

## Komodo National Park, Indonesia

A ferocious Komodo dragon flicks its long, forked tongue on the shores of its island home. The dragons are found only on several small islands in Indonesia, most of which are included in the national park.

### Abruzzo National Park, Italy

Goat-like animals called chamois *(SHAM ee)* peer down from their mountain perch in the park, located in the Apennine Mountains. Chamois once were common throughout the mountains of Europe.

# Poisoned Earth, Water, and Air

When insect pests damage such plants as cabbage (above), gardeners often spray the plants with pesticide. The pesticide settles on the leaves of the plants and gets into the bodies of insects, killing them. People or animals who eat the plants can get pesticide inside their bodies as well. Over time, the pesticide may make them sick.

Mr. Jones was worried. He had found some big green caterpillars munching on two of the cabbages in his garden. If he didn't protect his plants, insects might destroy them all.

So Mr. Jones bought some cans of chemicals called pesticide. This is a poison that kills insects and other pests. Mr. Jones sprayed the pesticide over his garden. Many of his neighbors used pesticide on their plants, too.

The pesticide seemed to work well. A cabbage moth fluttered down to lay her eggs on one of Mr. Jones's cabbages. The moth quickly died. But so did a lot of harmless insects—insects that could have been used as food by the birds.

Each time it rained, a lot of the pesticide washed off the plants and soaked into the ground where earthworms lived. As the worms crawled about on their earthworm business, eating their way through the soil, the pesticide got into their bodies. It didn't kill them, but they soon had a lot of it in their bodies.

One morning, a bright-breasted robin spied a worm in Mr. Jones's yard. The worm quickly became the robin's breakfast. Next morning, the robin was back again to catch another worm. This was a good place to hunt, so the robin began to come every day. Other robins came, too.

Pesticides also soak into the ground and get into the bodies of earthworms. Robins and other small birds that eat the worms get pesticide in their bodies. Too much can kill them.

One day when Mr. Jones came out to weed his garden, he found a dead robin lying in the grass. Sadly, he dug a small hole and buried the bird. He wondered what had killed it.

The robin had been poisoned. It was poisoned by the pesticide Mr. Jones and his neighbors had sprayed. The worms in the ground were filled with pesticide. When the robin ate the worms, the pesticide went into its body. After a while there was so much pesticide in the robin that it died.

There was trouble in other places, too. Gardeners and farmers for miles around had sprayed their gardens, lawns, and crops with pesticide. Rain washed a lot of the pesticide into nearby streams that flowed into a small lake. Soon there was a lot of pesticide in the lake. The bodies of the fish and other creatures that lived in the lake were filled with this poison.

A flock of large birds called ospreys lived near the lake. They swooped over the water, catching fish that swam near the top. The more fish the ospreys ate, the more pesticide got into their bodies.

The pesticide did not kill the ospreys. But it did cause changes inside their bodies. When it came time for the female

ospreys to lay eggs, the changes in their bodies made them lay eggs with shells so thin they would nearly all break, killing the chicks inside. Instead of a dozen or so new little ospreys to help the flock grow, there were only a few.

One of the pesticides that causes trouble like this is called DDT. For many years, farmers all over the world used DDT to protect their crops from hungry insects. It was also used to kill insects that cause diseases such as malaria and sleeping sickness. If it were not for DDT, millions of people would have suffered and died from these diseases.

Pesticides also get into streams, lakes, and ponds and then into the bodies of fish. Ospreys and other birds that eat the fish absorb pesticides into their bodies. The pesticide may not kill the ospreys, but it causes them to lay eggs that break more easily, killing the babies inside. Fewer osprey chicks are born.

At a power station in China, smoke pollutes the air for miles around, and chemicals foul the water.

A lot of DDT was used. It soaked into the earth and water everywhere in the world. People in most parts of the world stopped using DDT after the 1970's. But where DDT is still in the earth and water, it will cause trouble for a long time to come. Many new pesticides are now being used, but some of these are just as harmful to wildlife as DDT. Some pesticides must be used, so scientists are trying to find kinds that work well but do not harm wildlife.

Pesticides are only one kind of pollution that causes trouble for animals. There are other kinds of pollution that cause trouble, too. Chimneys and car engines fill the air with smoke. This smoke is made of different kinds of gases mixed with millions of tiny bits of rock and metal. Most of these gases are poisonous. This dirty air can make animals, plants, and people sick. It can even kill them.

Lakes and rivers are polluted by sewage from towns and cities and by fertilizer and livestock waste that run off of farms. (Fertilizers help farmers grow more crops to feed more people, but they also poison water.) An even worse kind of pollution comes from factories that dump used chemicals into lakes and rivers. Many of these chemicals poison the water so that animals cannot drink it. Creatures that live in the water are killed by the poisons.

Big, ocean-going ships called tankers carry oil from one place to another. Offshore drilling rigs drill through the ocean bottom to reach oil beneath the sea floor. In both cases, accidents sometimes happen, and huge quantities of oil spill into the ocean. If the leak cannot be stopped, great oil slicks form at the surface of the ocean. Many kinds of fish and other water creatures have been poisoned or killed by these giant oil slicks.

Volunteers clean tar from a beach in Florida after a massive oil spill in the Gulf of Mexico in 2010. The oil polluted water and beaches for miles around and killed many fish, birds, and other kinds of wildlife.

Sometimes the oil floats in toward the shore. Then the oil slick is a threat to sea birds. Auks, gulls, cormorants, ducks, and other fish-eating birds dive into the water to get their food. When they dive into an oil slick, the oil covers their feathers. Then the birds can no longer swim or fly. They are faced with a slow death. Hundreds of thousands of sea birds have been killed in this way.

If pollution is such a dreadful problem, what are we doing about it? Many farmers have begun to use natural ways to control pests and fertilize the soil. They use the natural enemies of insect pests to control harmful insects and rotate the crops they grow in various fields so that certain crops don't use up all of the nutrients in the soil.

More and more factories have machinery to clean up the smoke that comes from their furnaces. They use such technology as wind and solar power, which are renewable, cleaner resources. Many countries are working to clean up polluted rivers and lakes. Manufacturers are putting special equipment on cars and trucks to clean up the gases they release into the air. New cars have been developed to run on electricity, reducing the use of gas and oil.

Pollution is still a threat to wild animals, plants, and people. But we are trying to reduce and control it.

A teacher helps her
students collect samples
of sea water so that they
can test it for pollution.

# Helping Animals in Danger

*"When you have seen one ant, one bird, one tree, you have not seen them all. What is happening to the rain forests of Madagascar and Brazil will affect us all."*

**Edward O. Wilson**
An American biologist who studied how animals behave in groups, Wilson helped found the field of sociobiology. Sociobiologists study the ways heredity influences how animals behave.

# A Helping Hand for Whoopers

The small group of men stood on the muddy shore of a shallow lagoon. With anxious eyes, they looked into the sky.

Suddenly, one of the men pointed. "Here they come!" The men could just make out two black dots moving toward them—still high in the sky and far away. As the shapes came closer, the men could see two large, white birds clearly. Flying through the air with steadily beating wings, they were as swift and graceful as ballet dancers. Then, with their great, black-tipped wings stiffly outstretched, the birds skimmed down to land easily in the shallow water.

The first members of the whooping crane flock had returned to their winter home. They were back at the Aransas National Wildlife Refuge on the coast of Texas.

The men continued to watch the sky. Would all the cranes who had left in the spring come safely back? Had any new ones hatched during the summer?

"Here come two more. They have a young one!"

During the next few weeks, more cranes continued to arrive. Finally, they were all back. This time there were a few hundred of them—one of only three flocks of wild whooping cranes in the world.

Once, there had been several thousand cranes and several flocks. They went flapping northward each spring and came soaring back south each fall. The birds spent their summers on the lakes and ponds of Canada, Minnesota, North Dakota, Iowa, and Illinois. They mated and built nests among the cattails. They laid eggs and raised their babies.

In the autumn, the cranes and their young ones returned to the swamps and marshes of Florida, Texas, and Louisiana. This had been their way of life for half a million years.

But there came a time when the land began to change. People came in greater and greater numbers. They built houses and turned vast sections of wild prairie into farmland. Towns sprang up on the shores of lakes where cranes built their nests. Soon, there was not enough room for the cranes.

There were also new enemies— hunters with guns and people who collected birds' eggs for fun. Hundreds of cranes were killed and hundreds of eggs were taken from nests, never to hatch.

By the 1890's, whooping cranes were seldom seen in the places they once had lived. By 1930, there were no whooping cranes to be seen anywhere. Most scientists were sure they had become extinct.

But in 1936, a scientist named Neil Hotchkiss discovered that the cranes were not extinct. He found 4 of them. They were living on a small bit of marshland on the Texas coast.

Other scientists became interested. They found that there were 18 whooping cranes living in the marshland. It was the last winter home for the last flock of whooping cranes in the world.

Many people soon offered to help save the birds. The United States government bought the bit of land and turned it into a protected place where the birds would be safe. It became known as the Aransas National Wildlife Refuge. Scientists were put in charge of it, to study the whooping cranes and help protect them. With the help of the people who work at the refuge, the whooping crane flock survived. By 2010, it contained 216 birds. More whooping cranes lived in captivity in

several places in the United States and Canada.

In 1993, scientists began releasing young captive whooping cranes at Kissimmee Prairie in Florida. The first wild chicks in the group hatched in 2000. The small group lives in Florida year-round and does not migrate.

Whooping cranes learn about migration from their parents. In autumn 2001, scientists decided to teach a group of captive-born whooping cranes in Wisconsin how to migrate. They dressed in whooping crane costumes and flew in a specially designed aircraft. They led the whooping crane flock from their Wisconsin refuge to another refuge in Florida. Scientists led the cranes in this way for several years. In 2006, the first wild chicks hatched in Wisconsin.

Even though whooping cranes are doing better, they are still in danger. Something could easily happen to wipe them all out. However, the whooping crane *has* been saved, for a while at least. And this shows that maybe something *can* be done for all the world's vanishing animals.

# Chimpanzee Friends

Pooch—Olly—Goblin—David Graybeard—and old Mr. Worzle. These are some of the names that Jane Goodall gave to her wild chimpanzee friends.

Jane Goodall is a scientist. For many years she lived with wild chimpanzees in a forest in Africa. For the first six months, the chimps ran away whenever they saw her. But slowly they grew used to her. In time, some of them even became friendly.

She found that the chimps sometimes hunt and kill other animals for food. She saw that they often make very simple tools. And she found that each chimpanzee is different from every other chimpanzee—just as people are different from each other.

Jane Goodall wrote several books about her friends, the wild chimpanzees. She described how these smart animals are being hunted and pushed out of the places where they live. She said that this is a terrible thing, because we can learn much about ourselves by studying chimpanzees. But to do this, we need to study the chimps where they live—not in zoos.

Many scientists became interested in the work Jane Goodall did with chimpanzees. Other people who were interested in saving these animals collected money to start special parks in Africa. Here chimpanzees can be protected from people. They can live as they have always lived.

# The Crocodile Hunter

It's much easier to convince people to help animals when the animals are cute or beautiful. The thought of losing koala bears or whooping cranes forever makes people sad. They are willing to spend time or money to help the animals survive. Animals that are not cute—or those that frighten people—are a different story. It is harder to convince people that these animals should be saved, too. Yet that is what Steve Irwin devoted his life to doing—helping such animals as crocodiles and snakes and trying to convince other people to do the same.

Irwin was born in Australia. There, his parents established the Beerwah Reptile Park. (Reptiles are animals with dry, scaly skin, such as crocodiles, lizards, snakes, and turtles.) Irwin's mother nursed injured or orphaned wild animals and returned them to the wild. Irwin's father was often called upon to capture crocodiles or snakes that had wandered into areas where people lived and move the animals to safer locations. At the age of 9, Irwin began helping his father. He learned to wrestle small crocodiles and to safely handle all kinds of snakes.

As Irwin grew up, animals became his passion. The government of Queensland asked for his help in moving saltwater crocodiles from inhabited areas. Saltwater crocodiles are the biggest crocs in the world. They can reach lengths up to 23 feet (7 meters). Irwin relocated them or housed them in the Crocodile Environmental Park that his family established.

Eventually, Irwin took over his family's park and renamed it the Australia Zoo. He made movies that taught people about animals and urged them to save wildlife.

Irwin died in 2006, while filming a movie aboard his boat, *Croc One*. A poisonous barb at the end of the long tail of a fish called a stingray pierced his chest. Irwin once said, "My job, my mission, the reason I've been put on this planet, is to save wildlife." Now, his wife, Terri, and his children, Bindi and Robert, continue his work.

# A Refuge for Raptors

The tiny great horned owl chick was cold and hungry. For hours it had cried for its mother to come back to the nest and feed it. But she never came. Finally, the chick climbed out onto a nearby branch. Maybe now its mother would hear it. Instead, the little owl lost its footing and, because it couldn't fly yet, fell to the forest floor below. It huddled among some leaves throughout the night.

The next day, a woman walking her dog found the chick. She wrapped it in her sweater and drove it to a place she knew, where people take care of birds that are sick or hurt. There, the little owl was placed in a nest with Hootie, a wise old great horned owl that had never had chicks of her own.

Hootie kept the chick warm. When she heard its begging call, she fed it. As the chick grew, it learned everything it would need to know from Hootie. When it grew up, the chick was able to fly off on its own into the wild.

But Hootie was not alone for long. Soon, another orphaned chick was placed in her nest. In all, Hootie raised more than 300 great horned owl chicks over many years until she died in 2000. She was at least 34 years old.

The place where Hootie lived is called The Raptor Trust. It stands at the edge of the Great Swamp National Wildlife Refuge, near Meyersville, New Jersey. The Trust, a hospital for raptors and other birds, was started by self-taught *ornithologist* (bird expert) Leonard Soucy.

Raptors are birds of prey, a group that includes eagles, falcons, hawks, and owls. Such birds have large eyes, hooked beaks, and sharp claws. They soar high in the air, watching for such prey as rabbits, squirrels, and fish. They swoop down, grasp the animal in their strong claws, and carry it back to a perch or nest to eat.

At one time, people shot and poisoned raptors. But Soucy believed that all animals have a role to play in nature. He and his wife began to take in injured raptors. They kept the birds in their backyard. When the birds were well, they released them back into the wild.

Soon, the Soucys had more birds than there was room for. Some birds would never be able to take care of themselves. The Soucys built large, airy cages for such birds and allowed people to see them and learn about raptors. In 1982, the Soucys established The Raptor Trust. As more people offered to help, they were able to build larger facilities. Today, the Trust takes care of thousands of birds each year. Tens of thousands of people visit the education center. They leave with a greater respect for these once-misunderstood birds.

# What You Can Do

*"Only if we understand can we care. Only if we care will we help. Only if we help shall they be saved."*

**Jane Goodall**
An English zoologist whose work with chimpanzees revolutionized scientists' understanding of these animals, Goodall devoted her life to ensuring the survival of chimpanzees in the wild.

There are many things you, your friends, and your family can do to help all kinds of animals. One of the ways you can help animals most is just by leaving them alone! You can learn a lot about animals—and enjoy some of their funny ways—by watching them from a distance. Try observing one particular animal quietly for a while and see what you can learn. A pair of binoculars will allow you to get close to an animal without hurting or frightening it.

## Camping, fishing, hunting, or picnicking

Don't capture such small creatures as garter snakes, frogs, and turtles for pets. Leave them in the wild where they can live, have babies, and do their part to keep nature in balance.

Don't kill animals such as snakes and spiders just because you don't like them or because you fear them. Most of these animals are harmless to people. They also play an important part in keeping things in balance.

Obey the hunting and fishing laws. Don't overhunt or overfish—many animals are in trouble because of this.

## Vacationing

Don't take animals of any kind, or anything that might have insect eggs in it, from one part of the world to another. This often causes serious trouble to plant and animal life.

## Around the house

If you can, put a birdhouse or bird
feeder in your yard. Find out what
kind of food the birds in your area eat
and provide it for them.

Don't use weedkillers or other garden sprays that contain poisons that
may pollute the earth and nearby
ponds. Such sprays can kill many useful insects and can poison worms and
fish. They can even cause the death
of birds and other small animals.

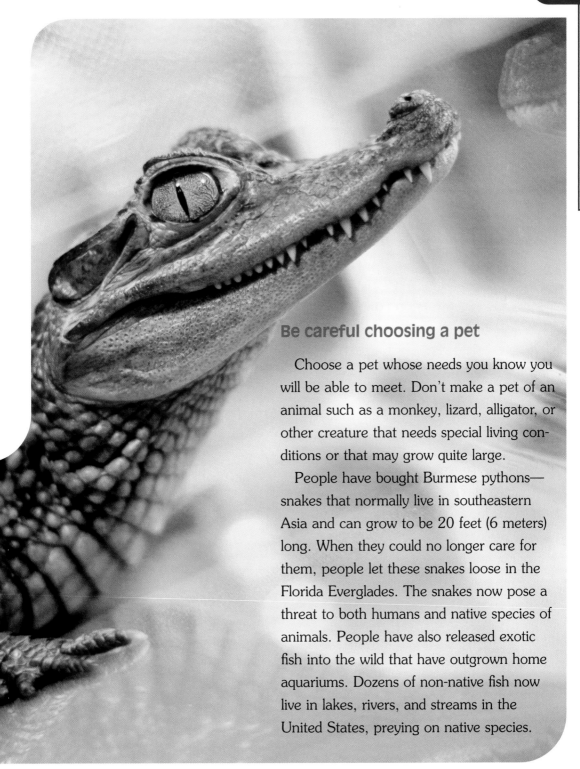

## Be careful choosing a pet

Choose a pet whose needs you know you will be able to meet. Don't make a pet of an animal such as a monkey, lizard, alligator, or other creature that needs special living conditions or that may grow quite large.

People have bought Burmese pythons— snakes that normally live in southeastern Asia and can grow to be 20 feet (6 meters) long. When they could no longer care for them, people let these snakes loose in the Florida Everglades. The snakes now pose a threat to both humans and native species of animals. People have also released exotic fish into the wild that have outgrown home aquariums. Dozens of non-native fish now live in lakes, rivers, and streams in the United States, preying on native species.

# Find out More

## Books to read

There are many exciting and interesting children's books about endangered animals, conservation, and ecology. You can find them in your school, public library, or book store. Here are just a few:

*Almost Gone: The World's Rarest Animals* by Steve Jenkins (HarperCollins, 2006)

*The Atlas of Endangered Animals* by Paula Hammond (Marshall Cavendish, 2010)

*The Buffalo Are Back* by Jean Craighead George (Dutton Children's Books, 2010)

*The Chimpanzees I Love* by Jane Goodall (Scholastic Press, 2001)

*Gorillas in Danger* by Helen Orme (Bearport Publishing, 2007)

*Grizzly Bears* by Jacqueline Dembar Greene (Bearport Publishing, 2008)

*Mass Extinction: Examining the Current Crisis* by Tricia Andryszewski (Twenty-First Century Books, 2008)

*The Penguin Problem* by Abby Klein (Scholastic, 2010)

*Planet Animal: Saving Earth's Disappearing Animals* by Barbara Taylor and Michael Chinery (Barron's, 2009)

*Tracks of a Panda* by Nick Dowson (Candlewick Press, 2007)

*The Wolves Are Back* by Jean Craighead George (Dutton Children's Books, 2008)

## Conservation groups

These are some of the major organizations that are working to help protect endangered animals. Check their websites for descriptions and contact information.

http://www.iucnredlist.org/

A group of scientists called the International Union for Conservation of Nature and Natural Resources maintains a website that keeps track of which animals are in danger and which are not. The website is called the IUCN Red List of Threatened Species.

## United States

**Izaak Walton League**
http://www.iwla.org/

Many local chapters work to protect our natural environment, including wildlife areas.

**National Audubon Society**
http://www.audubon.org/

Focuses on birds and protecting their habitats through a national network of nature centers, research groups, and educational programs.

**National Wildlife Federation**
http://www.nwf.org/

Promotes public interest and education in the conservation of wildlife and their habitats; publishes *Ranger Rick,* a magazine for children.

**Sierra Club**
http://www.sierraclub.org/

Takes a "hands-on" approach to conservation with projects and outings for people of all ages.

### The Wilderness Society
http://wilderness.org/

Works to place and keep millions of acres of forests, deserts, wetlands, and other natural areas under the protection of the United States government.

### World Wildlife Fund
http://www.worldwildlife.org/

Maintains projects around the world to actively protect threatened wildlife areas.

## Canada

### Canadian Wildlife Service
http://www.cws-scf.ec.gc.ca/nwrc-cnrf/

This agency of Canada's federal government runs the National Wildlife Research Centre, which keeps track of migrating birds and wildlife populations and diseases.

### ELSA Canada
http://www.elsacanada.com/

Works to save Canada's endangered wildlife mainly by helping to establish wildlife reserves.

### Nature Canada
http://www.naturecanada.ca/

Speaks out to improve conditions in national parks, helps endangered species, and solves pollution issues.

## United Kingdom

### Marine Conservation Society
http://www.mcsuk.org/

Promotes public support for healthy fishing areas, marine wildlife protection, and cleaning up the seas and shorelines.

### Royal Society for the Protection of Birds
http://www.rspb.org.uk/

Encourages volunteers, including youth, to help protect birds and their habitats.

## Australia

### Australian Conservation Foundation
http://www.acfonline.org.au/

Acts as a voice for a healthy environment in Australia by working with businesses, communities, and the national government.

### Wildlife Preservation Society of Australia
http://www.wpsa.org.au/

Offers educational and volunteer opportunities with the aim of keeping Australia's natural areas unharmed and preventing the extinction of any organism.

## New Zealand

### Forest & Bird
http://www.forestandbird.org.nz/

New Zealand's largest conservation organization works to preserve the country's natural heritage and native plants and animals.

### New Zealand Biodiversity
http://biodiversity.govt.nz/

A government agency responsible for maintaining a healthy balance among species living in New Zealand.

## South Africa

### Endangered Wildlife Trust
http://www.ewt.org.za/

Focuses on rebuilding the populations of endangered animals in South Africa and its surrounding ocean, such as the African crane and the riverine rabbit.

### WESSA (Wildlife and Environment Society of South Africa)
http://www.wessa.org.za/

A watchdog and educator for the wise management of South Africa's environment.

# Index

This index is an alphabetical list of important topics covered in words or pictures in this book. The index shows you what page or pages the information is on. For example, if you want to find out about a particular animal, such as the Bengal tiger, look under *Bengal tiger* or *tiger*. You will find a group of words called an entry, like this: Bengal tiger, 56-59 *(with pictures)*. This entry tells you that you can read about Bengal tigers on pages 56-59. The words *with pictures* tell you that there are pictures of Bengal tigers on these pages, too.

**A**

**Abruzzo National Park** (Italy), 173 *(with picture)*
**addax,** 54-55 *(with picture)*
**Africa**
  Maasai Mara Game Reserve (Kenya), 168 *(with picture)*
  vanishing animals
    addax, 54-55 *(with picture)*
    chimpanzee, 29, 38-41 *(with pictures)*, 61, 188-189 *(with picture)*
    dog, African wild, 46-47 *(with picture)*
    gorilla, lowland, 48-49 *(with picture)*
    ibis, northern bald, 50-51 *(with picture)*
    indri, 42-43 *(with picture)*
    rhinoceros, black, 52-53 *(with picture)*
    tortoise, geometric, 44-45 *(with picture)*
**African elephant,** 73, 168 *(with picture)*
**African wild dog,** 46-47 *(with picture)*
**albatross, Antipodean,** 140-141 *(with picture)*
**Amazon rain forest,** 162 *(picture)*
**American buffalo,** 170 *(with picture)*
**American mink,** 95
**amphibians,** 26 *(picture)*
  frog, 34-37
    golden poison, 132-133 *(with picture)*
**animals**
  number of species, 26
  "outsider," 163-164
  *see also* **extinct animals; vanishing animals**
**Antarctica,** 143
**Antipodean albatross,** 140-141 *(with picture)*
**Aransas National Wildlife Refuge,** 185, 186
**armadillo, giant,** 124-125 *(with picture)*
**Asia**
  parks and reserves
    Komodo National Park (Indonesia), 172 *(with picture)*
    Woolong National Nature Reserve (China), 171 *(with picture)*
  vanishing animals
    dolphin, Ganges, 68-69 *(with picture)*
    elephant, Asian, 72-73 *(with picture)*
    horse, wild, 29, 66-67 *(with picture)*
    Komodo dragon, 64-65 *(with picture)*, 172 *(with picture)*
    orangutan, 60-61 *(with picture)*, 160-161 *(with picture)*
    panda, giant, 70-71 *(with picture)*, 171 *(with picture)*
    snow leopard, 62-63 *(with picture)*, 159 *(picture)*
    tiger, Bengal, 56-59 *(with pictures)*
**Asian elephant,** 72-73 *(with picture)*
**asteroid,** 17
**Australia**
  Great Barrier Reef Marine Park, 166 *(with picture)*
  Steve Irwin's work, 190-191 *(with picture)*
  vanishing animals
    finch, Gouldian, 82-83 *(with picture)*
    numbat, 78-79 *(with picture)*
    Tasmanian devil, 74-77 *(with pictures)*
    wallaby, banded hare-, 84-85 *(with picture)*
    wombat, hairy-nosed, 80-81 *(with picture)*
**Australia Zoo,** 191

**B**

**Baird's tapir,** 130-131 *(with picture)*, 169 *(with picture)*
**balance of nature,** 155, 157, 197
**bald eagle,** 109
**bald ibis, northern,** 50-51 *(with picture)*
**bamboo,** 71
**banded hare-wallaby,** 84-85 *(with picture)*
**Banff National Park** (Canada), 167 *(with picture)*
**bat, Florida bonneted,** 104-105 *(with picture)*
**bear,** 71
  polar, 28-29 *(with pictures)*, 102-103 *(with picture)*, 157
  spectacled, 128-129 *(with picture)*
**Beerwah Reptile Park** (Australia), 191
**Bengal tiger,** 56-59 *(with pictures)*
**Bialowieza Forest,** 87-89
**bird feeders,** 198 *(with picture)*
**birds,** 17, 26 *(picture)*, 31
  albatross, Antipodean, 140-141 *(with picture)*
  condor, California, 114-115 *(with picture)*
  crane, whooping, 110-111 *(with picture)*, 184-187 *(with pictures)*
  dodo, 20-21 *(with picture)*
  eagle
    bald, 109
    golden, 109
  finch, Gouldian, 82-83 *(with picture)*

ibis, northern bald, 50-51 *(with picture)*
osprey, 175-176 *(with picture)*
owl, horned, 192-193 *(with picture)*
pelican, Dalmatian, 96-97 *(with picture)*
penguin, northern rockhopper, 142-143
     *(with picture)*
pigeon, passenger, 24-25 *(with picture)*
raptor, 192-193 *(with picture)*
robin, 175-176 *(with picture)*
woodpecker, ivory-billed, 116-117 *(with
     picture)*
wren, Stephens Island, 163
**bison,** 170 *(with picture)*
   *See also* **wisent**
**black-footed ferret,** 106-107 *(with picture)*
**black rhinoceros,** 52-53 *(with picture)*
**black-tailed prairie dog,** 107
**blue buck,** 22-23 *(with picture)*
**blue whale,** 144-145 *(with picture)*
**bonneted bat, Florida,** 104-105 *(with picture)*
**brown spider monkey,** 122-123 *(with picture)*
**buffalo, American,** 170 *(with picture)*
   *see also* **wisent**
**Burmese python,** 199

**C**
**California condor,** 114-115 *(with picture)*
**canine distemper,** 109
**Carson, Rachel,** 31
**Central America,** 121, 131, 169
**chamois,** 173 *(with picture)*
**Channel Islands,** 109
**chimpanzee,** 29, 38-41 *(with pictures)*, 61,
     188-189 *(with picture)*
**China,** 71, 171 *(with picture)*, 178-179
     *(picture)*
**chinchilla,** 126-127 *(with picture)*
**condor, California,** 114-115 *(with picture)*
**conservation, wildlife.** *See* **wildlife
     conservation**
**coral reef,** 166 *(with picture)*
**Corcovado National Park** (Costa Rica), 169
     *(with picture)*
**Corwin, Jeff,** 147
**coyote,** 101
**crane, whooping,** 110-111 *(with picture)*,
     184-187 *(with pictures)*
**crocodile,** 157
     saltwater, 190-191 *(with picture)*
**Crocodile Environmental Park,** 191

**D**
**Dalmatian pelican,** 96-97 *(with picture)*
**DDT,** 51, 177, 179
**deer,** 34, 57-58 *(with picture)*, 99-100
**devil, Tasmanian,** 74-77 *(with pictures)*
**devil facial tumor disease,** 77
**dinosaurs,** 8 *(picture)*, 16-17 *(with picture)*
**dodo,** 20-21 *(with picture)*

**dog, African wild,** 46-47 *(with picture)*
**dolphin**
   Ganges, 68-69 *(with picture)*
   river, 69

**E**
**eagle**
   bald, 109
   golden, 109
**echolocation,** 105
**elephant,** 157-158 *(with picture)*
   African, 73, 168 *(with picture)*
   Asian, 72-73 *(with picture)*
**elk,** 167 *(with picture)*
**endangered species,** 27
   *see also* **vanishing animals**
**Europe**
   Abruzzo National Park (Italy), 173 *(with
        picture)*
   vanishing animals
      chamois, 173 *(with picture)*
      lynx, Spanish, 90-91 *(with picture)*
      mink, European, 94-95 *(with picture)*
      pelican, Dalmatian, 96-97 *(with picture)*
      seal, Mediterranean monk, 92-93
           *(with picture)*
      wisent, 86-89 *(with pictures)*
**European mink,** 94-95 *(with picture)*
**extinct animals,** 8-9 *(with pictures)*
   blue buck, 22-23 *(with picture)*
   dinosaurs, 8 *(picture)*, 16-17 *(with picture)*
   dodo, 20-21 *(with picture)*
   passenger pigeon, 24-25 *(with picture)*
   quagga, 10-15 *(with picture)*, 29
   sea cow, Steller's, 18-19 *(with picture)*
   wren, Stephens Island, 163
**extinction**
   causes, 17
   defined, 27
   numbers of plants and animals, 26-27

**F**
**ferret**
   black-footed, 106-107 *(with picture)*
   domestic, 107
**fertilizer,** 179
**Field Museum** (Chicago), 16 *(picture)*
**finch, Gouldian,** 82-83 *(with picture)*
**fin whale,** 156 *(picture)*
**fish,** 27 *(picture)*
**fishing,** 197
**Florida bonneted bat,** 104-105 *(with picture)*
**forests, clearing of,** 161-163 *(with picture)*
**fox**
   island, 108-109 *(with picture)*
   red, 79
**frog,** 34-37
   golden poison, 132-133 *(with picture)*

**G**
**Ganges dolphin,** 68-69 *(with picture)*
**gemsbok,** 14
**geometric tortoise,** 44-45 *(with picture)*
**giant armadillo,** 124-125 *(with picture)*
**giant kangaroo rat,** 112-113 *(with picture)*
**giant panda,** 70-71 *(with picture),* 171
    *(with picture)*
**golden eagle,** 109
**golden lion tamarin,** 134-135 *(with picture)*
**golden poison frog,** 132-133 *(with picture)*
**Goodall, Jane,** 188-189 *(with picture),* 195
**gorilla,** 61
   lowland, 48-49 *(with picture)*
   mountain, 49
**Gouldian finch,** 82-83 *(with picture)*
**gray wolf,** 100
**Great Barrier Reef Marine Park** (Australia),
    166 *(with picture)*
**Gulf of Mexico oil spill,** 180 *(picture)*

**H**
**habitat,** 27
**hairy-nosed wombat,** 80-81 *(with picture)*
**hare-wallaby, banded,** 84-85 *(with picture)*
**Hootie** (owl), 192-193
**horned owl,** 192-193 *(with picture)*
**horse, wild,** 29, 66-67 *(with picture)*
**Hotchkiss, Neil,** 186
**hunting**
   by animals, 154-155 *(with picture)*
   by humans, 149-153 *(with pictures),*
     156-159 *(with pictures),* 197
   *see also by animal name*
**hyena,** 154-155 *(with picture)*

**I**
**ibis, northern bald,** 50-51 *(with picture)*
**indri,** 42-43 *(with picture)*
**insects,** 175, 197, 198
**International Union for Conservation of**
   **Nature and Natural Resources,** 26-27, 38
**International Whaling Commission,** 157
**invertebrates,** 26 *(picture)*
**Irwin, Steve,** 190-191 *(with picture)*
**island animals.** *See* **oceans and islands,**
   **vanishing animals of**
**island fox,** 108-109 *(with picture)*
**ivory,** 157-158 *(with picture)*
**ivory-billed woodpecker,** 116-117 *(with picture)*

**K**
**kangaroo,** 157
**kangaroo rat, giant,** 112-113 *(with picture)*
**killer whale,** 139

**Kissimmee Prairie** (Florida), 187
**Komodo dragon,** 64-65 *(with picture),*
    172 *(with picture)*
**Komodo Dragon National Park** (Indonesia),
    172 *(with picture)*

**L**
**laws.** *See* **wildlife conservation**
**leopard, snow,** 62-63 *(with picture),*
    159 *(picture)*
**Lord God Bird,** 117
**lowland gorilla,** 48-49 *(with picture)*
**lynx, Spanish,** 90-91 *(with picture)*

**M**
**Maasai Mara Game Reserve** (Kenya),
    168 *(with picture)*
**mammals,** 27 *(picture)*
   addax, 54-55 *(with picture)*
   armadillo, giant, 124-125 *(with picture)*
   bat, Florida bonneted, 104-105 *(with picture)*
   bear
     polar, 28-29 *(with pictures),* 102-103
      *(with picture),* 157
     spectacled, 128-129 *(with picture)*
   blue buck, 22-23 *(with picture)*
   buffalo, American (bison), 170 *(with picture)*
   chamois, 173 *(with picture)*
   chimpanzee, 29, 38-41 *(with pictures),* 61,
     188-189 *(with picture)*
   chinchilla, 126-127 *(with picture)*
   coyote, 101
   deer, 34, 57-58 *(with picture),* 99-100
   dog, African wild, 46-47 *(with picture)*
   dolphin, Ganges, 68-69 *(with picture)*
   elephant
     African, 73, 168 *(with picture)*
     Asian, 72-73 *(with picture)*
   elk, 167 *(with picture)*
   ferret
     black-footed, 106-107 *(with picture)*
     domestic, 107
   fox
     island, 108-109 *(with picture)*
     red, 79
   gemsbok, 14
   gorilla
     lowland, 48-49 *(with picture)*
     mountain, 49
   horse, wild, 29, 66-67 *(with picture)*
   hyena, 154-155 *(with picture)*
   indri, 42-43 *(with picture)*
   kangaroo, 157
   kangaroo rat, giant, 112-113 *(with picture)*
   lynx, Spanish, 90-91 *(with picture)*
   mink
     American, 95
     European, 94-95 *(with picture)*
   monkey, brown spider, 122-123 *(with picture)*

numbat, 78-79 *(with picture)*
orangutan, 60-61 *(with picture)*, 160-161
    *(with picture)*
otter, sea, 29, 136-139 *(with pictures)*
panda
    giant, 70-71 *(with picture)*, 171
        *(with picture)*
    red, 71
prairie dog, black-tailed, 107
quagga, 10-15 *(with picture)*, 29
quoll, 75-77
rhinoceros, 30 *(picture)*
    black, 52-53 *(with picture)*
sea cow, Steller's, 18-19 *(with picture)*
seal, Mediterranean monk, 92-93 *(with picture)*
snow leopard, 62-63 *(with picture)*,
    159 *(picture)*
tamarin, golden lion, 134-135 *(with picture)*
tapir, Baird's, 130-131 *(with picture)*,
    169 *(with picture)*
Tasmanian devil, 74-77 *(with pictures)*
tiger, Bengal, 56-59 *(with pictures)*
wallaby, banded hare-, 84-85 *(with picture)*
whale
    blue, 144-145 *(with picture)*
    fin, 156 *(picture)*
    killer, 139
wildebeest, 154-155 *(with picture)*
wisent, 86-89 *(with pictures)*
wolf
    gray, 100
    red, 98-101 *(with pictures)*
wombat, hairy-nosed, 80-81 *(with picture)*
zebra, 14
**Martha** (bird), 25
**Mediterranean monk seal,** 92-93 *(with picture)*
**mink**
    American, 95
    European, 94-95 *(with picture)*
**monkey, brown spider,** 122-123 *(with picture)*
**monk seal, Mediterranean,** 92-93 *(with picture)*
**mountain gorilla,** 49
**mud turtle,** 37

**N**
**national parks.** *See* **parks and reserves**
**North America**
    parks
        Banff National Park (Canada), 167 *(with*
            *picture)*
        Corcovado National Park (Costa Rica),
            169 *(with picture)*
        Yellowstone National Park (United States),
            170 *(with picture)*
    vanishing animals
        bat, Florida bonneted, 104-105 *(with*
            *picture)*
        bear, polar, 28-29 *(with pictures)*,
            102-103 *(with picture)*, 157

condor, California, 114-115 *(with picture)*
crane, whooping, 110-111 *(with picture)*,
    184-187 *(with pictures)*
ferret, black-footed, 106-107 *(with picture)*
fox, island, 108-109 *(with picture)*
kangaroo rat, giant, 112-113 *(with picture)*
wolf, red, 98-101 *(with pictures)*
woodpecker, ivory-billed, 116-117 *(with*
    *picture)*
**northern bald ibis,** 50-51 *(with picture)*
**northern rockhopper penguin,** 142-143 *(with*
    *picture)*
**numbat,** 78-79 *(with picture)*

**O**
**oceans and islands, vanishing animals of**
    albatross, Antipodean, 140-141 *(with picture)*
    otter, sea, 29, 136-139 *(with pictures)*
    penguin, northern rockhopper, 142-143 *(with*
        *picture)*
    tuatara, 164 *(with picture)*
    whale, blue, 144-145 *(with picture)*
    wren, Stephens Island, 163
**oil pollution,** 179-180 *(with picture)*
**orangutan,** 60-61 *(with picture)*, 160-161
    *(with picture)*
**osprey,** 175-176 *(with picture)*
**otter, sea,** 29, 136-139 *(with pictures)*
**owl, horned,** 192-193 *(with picture)*
**oyster,** 137

**P**
**panda**
    giant, 70-71 *(with picture)*, 171 *(with picture)*
    red, 71
**parks and reserves,** 157, 165-173 *(with*
    *pictures)*
**passenger pigeon,** 24-25 *(with picture)*
**pelican, Dalmatian,** 96-97 *(with picture)*
**penguin, northern rockhopper,** 142-143 *(with*
    *picture)*
**pesticides,** 174-177 *(with pictures)*, 179, 198
**pests, animals as,** 158, 175
**pets,** 199
**pigeon, passenger,** 24-25 *(with picture)*
**plants, extinction of,** 26
**poison frog, golden,** 132-133 *(with picture)*
**polar bear,** 28-29 *(with pictures)*, 102-103 *(with*
    *picture)*, 157
**pollution,** 174-181 *(with pictures)*, 198
**prairie dog,** 158
    black-tailed, 107
**Przewalski's horse.** *See* **wild horse**
**python, Burmese,** 199

**Q**
**quagga,** 10-15 *(with pictures)*, 29
**quoll,** 75-77

**R**
rain forest, 162 *(picture)*
raptor, 192-193 *(with picture)*
Raptor Trust, The, 193
red fox, 79
Red List, 27
red panda, 71
red wolf, 98-101 *(with pictures)*
reptiles, 27 *(picture)*
  conservation of, 191
  crocodile, 157
    saltwater, 190-191 *(with picture)*
  dinosaurs, 8 *(picture)*, 16-17 *(with picture)*
  Komodo dragon, 64-65 *(with picture)*,
    172 *(with picture)*
  python, Burmese, 199
  tortoise, geometric, 44-45 *(with picture)*
  tuatara, 164 *(with picture)*
  turtle, river, 118-121 *(with pictures)*
reserves. *See* **parks and reserves**
rhinoceros, 30 *(picture)*, 149-153 *(with*
    *pictures)*, 157-158
  black, 52-53 *(with picture)*
river dolphin, 69
river turtle, 118-121 *(with pictures)*
robin, 175-176 *(with picture)*
rockhopper penguin, northern, 142-143 *(with*
    *picture)*

**S**
Sahara, 55
saltwater crocodile, 190-191 *(with picture)*
San Diego Wild Animal Park, 165
sea cow, Steller's, 18-19 *(with picture)*
seal, Mediterranean monk, 92-93 *(with picture)*
sea otter, 29, 136-139 *(with pictures)*
*Silent Spring* (Carson), 31
snow leopard, 62-63 *(with picture)*,
    159 *(picture)*
Soucy, Leonard, 193
South America, vanishing animals of
  armadillo, giant, 124-125 *(with picture)*
  bear, spectacled, 128-129 *(with picture)*
  chinchilla, 126-127 *(with picture)*
  frog, golden poison, 132-133 *(with picture)*
  monkey, brown spider, 122-123 *(with picture)*
  tamarin, golden lion, 134-135 *(with picture)*
  tapir, Baird's, 130-131 *(with picture)*,
    169 *(with picture)*
  turtle, river, 118-121 *(with pictures)*
Spanish lynx, 90-91 *(with picture)*
spectacled bear, 128-129 *(with picture)*
spider monkey, brown, 122-123 *(with picture)*
Steller's sea cow, 18-19 *(with picture)*
Stephens Island wren, 163
Sue (skeleton), 16 *(picture)*

**T**
tamarin, golden lion, 134-135 *(with picture)*
tapir, Baird's, 130-131 *(with picture)*,
    169 *(with picture)*
Tasmanian devil, 74-77 *(with pictures)*
Thoreau, Henry David, 9
threatened species
  defined, 27
  numbers of, 26-27 *(with pictures)*
  *see also* **vanishing animals**
tiger, Bengal, 56-59 *(with pictures)*
tortoise, geometric, 44-45 *(with picture)*
tuatara, 164 *(with picture)*
turtle
  mud, 37
  river, 118-121 *(with pictures)*
*Tyrannosaurus rex,* 16 *(picture)*

**V**
vanishing animals, 26-27
  books to read, 200
  keeping track of, 28-29 *(with pictures)*
  threats to, 147 *(with picture)*
    changes in the land, 160-165 *(with pictures)*
    hunting, 149-153 *(with pictures)*,
      156-159 *(with pictures)*
  pollution, 174-181 *(with pictures)*
  ways of helping, *see* **wildlife conservation**
vanishing animals, names of
  addax, 54-55 *(with picture)*
  albatross, Antipodean, 140-141 *(with picture)*
  armadillo, giant, 124-125 *(with picture)*
  bat, Florida bonneted, 104-105 *(with picture)*
  bear
    polar, 102-103 *(with picture)*
    spectacled, 128-129 *(with picture)*
  chimpanzee, 29, 38-41 *(with pictures)*, 61,
    188-189 *(with picture)*
  chinchilla, 126-127 *(with picture)*
  condor, California, 114-115 *(with picture)*
  crane, whooping, 110-111 *(with picture)*,
    184-187 *(with pictures)*
  dog, African wild, 46-47 *(with picture)*
  dolphin, Ganges, 68-69 *(with picture)*
  elephant, Asian, 72-73 *(with picture)*
  ferret, black-footed, 106-107 *(with picture)*
  fox, island, 108-109 *(with picture)*
  frog, golden poison, 132-133 *(with picture)*
  gorilla, lowland, 48-49 *(with picture)*
  Gouldian finch, 82-83 *(with picture)*
  horse, wild, 66-67 *(with picture)*
  ibis, northern bald, 50-51 *(with picture)*
  indri, 42-43 *(with picture)*
  kangaroo rat, giant, 112-113 *(with picture)*
  Komodo dragon, 64-65 *(with picture)*,
    172 *(with picture)*
  lynx, Spanish, 90-91 *(with picture)*
  mink, European, 94-95 *(with picture)*
  monkey, brown spider, 122-123 *(with picture)*

numbat, 78-79 *(with picture)*
orangutan, 60-61 *(with picture)*
otter, sea, 136-139 *(with pictures)*
panda, giant, 70-71 *(with picture)*,
    171 *(with picture)*
pelican, Dalmatian, 96-97 *(with picture)*
penguin, northern rockhopper, 142-143
    *(with picture)*
rhinoceros, black, 52-53 *(with picture)*
seal, Mediterranean monk, 92-93 *(with
    picture)*
snow leopard, 62-63 *(with picture)*,
    159 *(picture)*
tamarin, golden lion, 134-135 *(with picture)*
tapir, Baird's, 130-131 *(with picture)*,
    169 *(with picture)*
Tasmanian devil, 74-77 *(with pictures)*
tiger, Bengal, 56-59 *(with pictures)*
tortoise, geometric, 44-45 *(with picture)*
turtle, river, 119-121 *(with pictures)*
wallaby, banded hare-, 84-85 *(with picture)*
whale, blue, 144-145 *(with picture)*
wisent, 86-89 *(with pictures)*
wolf, red, 98-101 *(with pictures)*
wombat, hairy-nosed, 80-81 *(with picture)*
woodpecker, ivory-billed, 116-117 *(with
    picture)*
**vulnerable species,** 27
*See also* **vanishing animals**

**W**
**wallaby, banded hare-,** 84-85 *(with picture)*
**whale,** 157
    blue, 144-145 *(with picture)*
    fin, 156 *(picture)*
    killer, 139
**whaling,** 145, 156-157 *(with picture)*
**white-nose syndrome,** 105
**whooping crane,** 110-111 *(with picture)*,
    184-187 *(with pictures)*
**wild dog, African,** 46-47 *(with picture)*
**wildebeest,** 47, 154-155 *(with picture)*
**wild horse,** 29, 66-67 *(with picture)*

**wildlife conservation,** 157, 165, 182-183
    *(with picture)*
    animals helped by
        bat, Florida bonneted, 105
        chimpanzee, 188-189 *(with picture)*
        condor, California, 115
        crane, whooping, 185-187 *(with pictures)*
        crocodile, saltwater, 190-191 *(with picture)*
        ferret, black-footed, 107
        finch, Gouldian, 83
        fox, island, 109
        horse, wild, 67
        mink, European, 95
        numbat, 79
        panda, giant, 71
        pelican, Dalmatian, 97
        penguin, northern rockhopper, 143
        raptor, 192-193 *(with picture)*
        Tasmanian devil, 77
        tuatara, 164 *(with picture)*
        wisent, 88-89
        wolf, red, 100-101
    groups, 200-201
    parks and reserves, 165-173 *(with pictures)*
    what you can do, 196-199 *(with pictures)*
**Wilson, Edward O.,** 183
**wisent,** 86-89 *(with pictures)*
**wolf**
    gray, 100
    red, 98-101 *(with pictures)*
**wombat, hairy-nosed,** 80-81 *(with picture)*
**woodpecker, ivory-billed,** 116-117 *(with picture)*
**Woolong National Nature Reserve** (China),
    171 *(with picture)*
**World Wildlife Fund,** 59
**wren, Stephens Island,** 163

**Y**
**Yellowstone National Park,** 170 *(with picture)*

**Z**
**zebra,** 14